Can Government Do Anything Right?

Democratic Futures series

Alasdair Roberts

———

Can Government Do Anything Right?

polity

First published in 2018 by Polity Press

Polity Press
65 Bridge Street
Cambridge CB2 1UR, UK

Polity Press
101 Station Landing
Suite 300
Medford, MA 02155, USA

ISBN-13: 978-1-5095-2150-0
ISBN-13: 978-1-5095-2151-7(pb)

A catalogue record for this book is available from the British Library.

Typeset in 11 on 15pt Sabon
by Fakenham Prepress Solutions, Fakenham, Norfolk NR21 8NN
Printed and bound in Great Britain by Clays Ltd, St. Ives PLC.

The publisher has used its best endeavours to ensure that the URLs for external websites referred to in this book are correct and active at the time of going to press. However, the publisher has no responsibility for the websites and can make no guarantee that a site will remain live or that the content is or will remain appropriate.

Every effort has been made to trace all copyright holders, but if any have been inadvertently overlooked the publisher will be pleased to include any necessary credits in any subsequent reprint or edition.

For further information on Polity, visit our website:
politybooks.com

Contents

Acknowledgments

I began this book while teaching at the Truman School of Public Affairs at the University of Missouri. My thinking on the subject was improved through conversations with students in my graduate seminar on governance and public affairs. I am particularly grateful to Kyoung-sun Min for helping me talk through ideas. I must also thank Dean Bart Wechsler for his collegiality and support during my time at the Truman School. A few words from Harry S. Truman, president of the United States from April 1945 to January 1953, make a fitting epigraph for the book, given its emphasis on the challenges of leadership in a turbulent world. "I discovered that being a president is like riding a tiger," Truman wrote in 1956. "A man has to keep on riding or be swallowed."

1

Why is Everyone so Angry?

So far as government is concerned, everything has just gone to hell. There does not seem to be much disagreement on this. In the United States, according to opinion polls, a large majority of people think that the country is heading in the wrong direction. They have believed this for years, and they blame it mainly on government. Government failed to prevent the financial crisis of 2008, and failed to achieve a speedy recovery afterward. It has failed to redress economic inequality and guarantee access to healthcare and other basic services. It seems incapable of controlling the inflow of people across borders. It bungles the response to major natural disasters. It entangles the country in ill-advised wars (in Iraq and Afghanistan) and ill-conceived military interventions (in Libya and Syria). It does nothing to control the growth of public debt or avert the cataclysm of climate change.

Can Government Do Anything Right?

Government, it appears, is a sprawling, dissolute, feckless disaster. No wonder that Americans express little faith in major public institutions. According to a 2016 Gallup Poll, only 10 percent of Americans had a lot of confidence in the US Congress. People are also increasingly dissatisfied with the presidency, major political parties, courts and the police, public schools, and the medical system. Since 2009, the country has been roiled with protests such as the Tea Party movement, Occupy Wall Street, and Black Lives Matter. In the 2016 presidential election, the early favorite (Hillary Clinton) had an unexpectedly tough race for the Democratic nomination against an outsider, the social democrat Bernie Sanders. This was followed by defeat in the general election at the hands of another outsider, Donald Trump, a man who had no government experience at all. Trump's election turned Washington politics upside down. He had a "100-day action plan to Make America Great Again." But at the end of those hundred days, most of Trump's promises were unfulfilled. Washington appeared to be as dysfunctional and gridlocked as ever.

The gloom has spread across the Atlantic. It took almost seventy years to build the institutions that now constitute the European Union. Over the decades, political leaders have developed sophisticated methods for removing barriers to movement between nations and rationalizing laws across the continent. However, this great project of continental integration seems to be at risk of collapse. Many people believe that the policies adopted by EU leaders in the wake of the 2007–8 financial crisis and the 2015–17 migrant crisis were ineffectual and even cruel. Harmony within the union has been displaced by rancor. Presidents and prime ministers snipe at one another and struggle to maintain authority at home. Left-wing populist movements have reached for power in Greece, Italy and Spain, while right-wing populists have done the same in Austria, Denmark, France, and the Netherlands.

"Things fall apart," the poet W.B. Yeats once wrote, "the center cannot hold." This is how politics felt in the United Kingdom in the years following the financial crisis. In a referendum held in June 2016, a slim majority of citizens voted for the UK to leave the European Union. Many leading politicians opposed the proposal, but this carried little weight. According to a 2016 Ipsos MORI poll, four out of five Britons do not trust politicians to tell the truth. Many want to "take their country back." But a solid majority in Scotland opposed exit from the European Union, and in March 2017 the Scottish Parliament called for another referendum on secession from the United Kingdom. Some Scots regard the British Parliament just as many English regard the European Parliament, and as many Americans regard their Congress: as alien and incompetent.

In France, anguish about the ineptitude of government in halting national decay resulted in the addition of a new word – *déclinisme* – to the French vocabulary. But there were *déclinistes* in other countries too. In the United States, the distinguished commentators Paul Krugman and Francis Fukuyama feared that their country was collapsing into a "failed state."[1] The *Financial Times* worried about a "real sickness in British and American democracy."[2] The researchers Roberto Stefan Foa and Yascha Mounk warned about "democratic breakdown" throughout North America and Western Europe.[3] Others think that we are witnessing the decline of Western civilization. "Some of the most fundamental pillars of the West and of the liberal international order are weakening," a German report warned in 2017. "Citizens of democracies believe less and less that their systems are able to deliver positive outcomes for them and increasingly favor national solutions and closed borders over globalism and openness."[4]

Why is Everyone so Angry?

Can government do *anything* right? This brief canvas of public and expert opinion might make us wonder. The purpose of this short book is to provide a framework for answering the question more precisely. It may also put our current worries in perspective. The following chapters will remind us what the basic functions of government are, and suggest that in fundamental ways Western countries are still strong performers. It will also argue that in some ways the problems preoccupying us today are enduring ones, and not portents of imminent collapse. Finally, and perhaps most importantly, the aim is to remind us that governing is extraordinarily difficult work, involving the constant adaptation of institutions and laws to suit a complex and turbulent world.

We must begin with a quick survey of some basic ideas. The fundamental unit of governance in the modern world is the state, a body recognized in international law that has jurisdiction over a defined territory and the people within it. There are 195 states in the world today. (That is an approximate number: there is debate among diplomats on whether the existence of a few should be acknowledged.) These 195 states assert authority over almost all the earth's surface. On average, each state governs 600,000 square kilometers of land and thirty million people. All states are bound together by customs and laws within a global system of states, sometimes also called the society of states. The keel of the modern state system was laid down in Europe about 400 years ago.

In every state, there are people who claim to be in charge. We used to call these people "rulers," and sometimes we still do, mainly when talking about states that are not democracies. For example, we often read about China's rulers, but rarely about the United States'. More often, we read about leaders, policymakers, or decision-makers in Western democracies. These are euphemisms. Whatever the word, we are talking about the people who exercise power within a state. These leaders have four goals, regardless of whether their states are democratic or non-democratic.

The first goal is the achievement of mastery over circumstances. Like everybody else, leaders dislike uncertainty. They want to know what is going on inside the borders of their territory, so that they can discourage behavior that threatens internal peace and order, and encourage behavior that advances the national interest. There is a similar desire for information about the plans of other states and foreigners, and an ambition to shape their behavior as well, with the aim of creating a state system that is stable and serves the national interest. But mastery over circumstances, whether internal or external, is elusive. It is constantly pursued but never fully achieved by any state.

The second goal is the attainment of legitimacy, or a general recognition of a state's right to govern its territory. This also has an internal and external aspect. A state must be respected by the people living within its borders, and by other states. There is a practical reason why legitimacy matters. Policymakers have a limited capacity to achieve compliance with their commands by force. Most of the time, people living within a state obey its laws because they think that is the right thing to do. Similarly, other countries are more likely to cooperate with a state's foreign policy, and refrain from attacking it, if they also recognize its right to exist and believe that it is behaving as a responsible member of the society of states.

The third goal is the advancement of human rights. We will define this concept later. Human rights are important as a matter of principle: we want leaders to pay attention to them even if self-interest would not push leaders in that direction. Increasingly, though, it is in the self-interest of leaders to respect human rights, or at least to appear respectful of them. It is hard to achieve legitimacy, either at home or abroad, while abusing fundamental rights. A governed population is more likely to resist commands, and other states are more likely to intervene in the internal affairs of a state, if its leaders seem to be maltreating their people.

The final goal for leaders is the promotion of economic growth. A strong and growing economy is essential for the achievement of all other objectives. Prosperity makes it easier to maintain internal order, because people are happier and less likely to fight each other if economic gains are widely distributed. Other countries also have an incentive to get along with a state if it has a thriving economy, because they will seek its largesse or access to its markets. A bigger economy also means more tax revenue, which improves the ability of leaders to police their own land, defend against attack, and provide services that advance human rights.

The simultaneous pursuit of these four goals is hard work, for several reasons. Leaders must make difficult trade-offs between goals. For example, a strong defense against external threats may require high taxes and conscription, which usually undermines public support for government. Similarly, a drive to maintain internal order might undermine human rights. Leaders also wrestle with uncertainty about tactics. The communities that they are trying to influence are vast and complex, and it is never clear which of several alternate lines of action is most likely to accomplish a specific goal. Machiavelli had this sort of uncertainty in mind when, in the early sixteenth century, he wondered whether it was better for a prince to be loved or feared. Machiavelli was struggling to determine which path was more likely to maintain the prince's power. We echo Machiavelli when we argue about the wisdom of zero-tolerance policing or the use of hard power in foreign policy.

Over time, the leaders of a state develop a broad strategy that establishes the relative importance of these four goals and lays out a path for pursuing them. When people talk about the "American way of life," they are describing the governance strategy pursued by one country, which emphasizes limited government, strong protection of a limited set of human rights, and free markets. In 2002, President George W. Bush argued that this was the "single sustainable model for national success."[5] Many people think that this is open to debate. When experts talk about the "China model," they are describing a very different governance strategy, one which emphasizes centralized government, weak protection for human rights, and extensive government intervention in the economy.

Throughout history, leaders have pursued many other governance strategies as well. We can make moral judgments about each of these strategies. We can also make purely practical judgments about which strategies will hold up in the long run – that is, about the survival prospects of a state that pursues one strategy or another.

Governance strategies begin as ideas, but they are articulated through institutions and laws. Leaders invest a lot of effort in building the institutions and drafting the laws that breathe life into a governance strategy. This process is referred to as institutional consolidation. It takes many years to construct institutions and laws, to persuade powerful interests that they should be taken seriously, and to educate the public about how they work. In the early years of the American republic, for example, policymakers established expansive civic education programs to promote "sympathy with our institutions and ideals," especially among immigrants. Similarly, Chinese policymakers have undertaken programs of "patriotic education" to promote the virtues of strong central government and leadership by the Communist Party. This labor does not end when institutions and laws are finally established. Institutions must also be administered, which is not easy. Sometimes institutions ignore the instructions given to them by leaders. Sometimes institutions break down and do nothing at all.

There is a final difficulty that complicates the work of designing and implementing governance strategies. Each strategy is tailored to fit the realities confronting a specific country at a specific moment in history. But we live in a turbulent world, and the domestic and international conditions that undergird a governance strategy never remain fixed. Power shifts within the society of states, people move around, industries rise and fall, and technologies evolve. We have even learned that climate and geography change over time. All of this means that governance strategies, and the institutions and laws that give life to those strategies, must be renovated constantly to fit new conditions. As John Dewey said, the design of any state is an experimental process: "Almost as soon as its form is stabilized, it needs to be re-made."[6]

It is easy to show that governance strategies do change dramatically over time. Thomas Jefferson would be stunned by the modern-day version of the "American way of life," which includes a vast military-industrial complex and alliances spanning the globe. Similarly, Mao Zedong would be appalled to see how free markets and private wealth are tolerated under the today's "China

11

model." In both cases, governance strategies have been adapted because leaders thought that they were ill-suited to new realities. This process of strategic adaptation can be slow and painful. It involves institutional *de*consolidation – that is, overcoming vested interests and changing public opinion so that outmoded institutions and laws can be torn down and rebuilt. People must be persuaded that yesterday's institutions and laws should not be taken so seriously after all, and educated about the need for new institutions and laws.

We are talking about the problems of statesmanship. Leaders must juggle competing objectives, gamble on the best ways of pursuing those objectives, and build up and tear down institutions and laws. And they must do this under conditions of unrelenting political, social, economic, and technological change. It is hard not to have sympathy with our leaders as they do this work. We could paraphrase Samuel Johnson here: modern governance may not be done well, but perhaps it is a surprise to see it done at all. Indeed, we shall see that in most of the world it is done very poorly. Leaders cannot formulate and execute strategies that advance the welfare of their people.

The remainder of this book explores a few of the challenges of governance in more detail. In the next chapter, we will look at the challenge of establishing peace and order, which is one aspect of the general project of achieving mastery over circumstances. I will argue that some recent tensions in European and American politics are related to this centuries-old challenge. Then we will look at the task of establishing legitimacy – another enduring problem, which leaders struggle constantly to manage. The same can be said about the problem of promoting economic growth, examined in Chapter 4: a tricky assignment because markets are constantly changing their shape.

The following two chapters focus on more recent events. In Chapter 5, I will examine a problem that has preoccupied leaders over the last forty years. This is the apparent tension between the principle of democratic control, which is a key technique for establishing legitimacy, and the drive to recover from the economic doldrums of the 1970s. The "neoliberal paradigm" (sometimes known as Reaganism or Thatcherism) was a strategy for managing this tension, but I will argue that it has exhausted its usefulness. In Chapter 6, I will look to the next thirty years, and describe the fundamental choice that must be made as we deal with terrorism, great power conflict, inequality, and climate change.

Can Government Do Anything Right?

In all these chapters, we will see leaders struggling to steer the ship of state. There are moments when the weather is fine and the ship of state sails smoothly with little need for direction. More often, the weather is rough and captaincy is more demanding. In the final chapter, I will argue that we are in a patch of rough weather right now. Ideas about governance whose soundness was generally acknowledged only a few years ago, now seem stale and outmoded. We see a need to abandon the status quo, but we are not sure what the new governance strategy should be. These moments of strategic change are difficult. They can generate deep anxieties about the future. But these moments are also unavoidable, and I will argue that democratic systems are better than most in responding constructively to them. The world is not falling apart, as the *déclinistes* would have you think. We are just inventing a new way forward.

2

The Long Peace

The Universal Declaration of Human Rights adopted by the United Nations in 1948 says that everyone has the right to "life, liberty, and security of person." It echoes the American Declaration of Independence of 1776, which announces the right to "life, liberty, and the pursuit of happiness." The drafters of the American declaration were influenced by the British philosopher John Locke, who wrote in 1689 that the purpose of government was to protect "life, liberty, and estate."

Today, we usually focus on the importance of liberty, but the first item in all these lists is life itself. The most fundamental of all human interests is protection against violence. The authors of the UN declaration knew this from experience. In 1948, they reflected on thirty years of war that caused eighty million deaths around the globe. The

15

authors of the American declaration lived through the Seven Years' War, a global conflict that caused more than one million deaths. (In the next forty years, another six million would die in European wars.) John Locke wrote in the wake of the English civil wars, the Scottish invasion of England, and the English conquest of Ireland, which resulted in a half million deaths. Locke also witnessed the end of the Thirty Years' War (1618–48), in which eight million Europeans died through combat, famine and disease.

There are large parts of the world that are like this today. Most modern states have only a tenuous hold on their territory. Often, struggles for power in these countries turn violent. One result is vast human misery. More than five million people died because of war within the Democratic Republic of Congo between 1998 and 2007. This struggle, involving twenty rebel groups and the armies of nine countries, has been called one of the "great human cataclysms of our time."[1] The Sri Lankan civil war, which lasted from 1983 to 2009, may have caused 100,000 deaths. A similar number were killed or injured as Russia fought with the breakaway republic of Chechnya between 1994 and 2009. A half million have died since the outbreak of civil war in Somalia in 1991. The Syrian civil war, which began in 2011, has also caused a half million deaths. Millions more are refugees, fleeing not only the military clashes but also the breakdown of social order across Syria.

The countries of the developed West, by contrast, are by and large at peace. Almost three generations of Westerners have grown up without knowing the trauma of war in their homelands. (The Yugoslav wars of the 1990s were a jarring exception.) Indeed, the era since World War II has been called "the long peace."[2] It is distinguished by a lack of war between Western states, the absence of civil and secessionist wars, and a decline in rates of violent crime. The frequency of terrorist attacks also has declined in the United States and Western Europe over the last four decades.[3] Professor Steven Pinker has argued that people in the West might be living "in the most peaceable era in our species' existence."[4]

Westerners take this peace for granted. Even when politics becomes fraught, we do not contemplate that it might degenerate into mass violence. Americans complain about polarization, but they do not worry about civil war or rebellion. The British voted to leave the European Union without fearing that an imbalance of power on the continent would lead to another general European war. No one expects that a vote for independence in Scotland would lead to English troops in Scottish streets. Similarly, the English do not fear that an independent Scotland will ally with European states to invade their homeland. It seems absurd to mention these possibilities. This is something that we should bear in mind when we judge how well our governments perform. In all preceding centuries, there were moments at which the leaders of the major Western states – including the United States – worried intensely about invasion, rebellion, and civil war. So far, the twenty-first century is the exception. This is a remarkable accomplishment.

This long peace has been achieved through a never-ending process of experimentation with different governance strategies. In Europe, we can mark three distinct phases in the evolution of such strategies. In the sixteenth and seventeenth centuries, major European states had a straight-forward formula for defending territory from attack by other states. They developed armies and navies that were professionally administered and good at technological innovation. European states were ready to fight. Indeed, they glorified combat, and responded quickly to provocations and slights to national honor. A reputation for militarism and tetchiness discouraged attacks. This approach to national security depended on the use of force internally as well. It required the imposition of taxes (which is simply a way of seizing private wealth) and the conscription of soldiers and sailors (which is a form of forced labor).

Statesmen eventually learned the weaknesses of this approach to national security. Above all, it did not produce a durable peace among states. Militarism and tetchiness might have been rational policies for individual countries, but they were not healthy for the entire society of European states, which found itself in a condition of almost continuous conflict throughout the seventeenth and eighteenth centuries.[5] Reliance on force also upset peace and order at home. Anger over war taxes contributed to the outbreak of civil wars in England and France in the 1600s, rebellions within the Habsburg Empire in the 1700s, the American rebellion of 1776–81, and the revolution in France in 1789. Conscription triggered riots and produced military forces that were plagued by desertion and mutiny.

Gradually, European states developed an alternative approach to peace among states. Force was tempered by diplomacy at home and abroad. Internally, monarchs negotiated political settlements with landowners that limited their ability to impose taxes, sometimes by requiring the approval of parliaments. Abroad, diplomats refined the balance-of-power system, a web of defensive alliances that was designed to discourage states from declaring war on one another. The system did not discourage militarism entirely. Countries still had to maintain standing forces and demonstrate their readiness to honor treaties. But the system was effective in reducing the amount of war in Europe in the nineteenth century, as well as the need for taxes and conscription.

This revised approach to peace broke down in 1914, plunging Europe into chaos on a scale not seen since the early 1600s. The pressures of war led to a great extension of government controls over everyday life. Societies were regimented so that they could fight wars more effectively. Governments taxed, borrowed, regulated, and conscripted more than ever before. The strain on domestic political arrangements was intense. In some countries, it led to revolution or dictatorship. In the United States and the United Kingdom, leaders tried to bolster domestic support by extending the right to vote and making promises about the extension of public services when war was over. This was the moment at which the idea of the "welfare state" was born.

In Europe, the decades following World War II have been absorbed with the pursuit of a third approach for avoiding interstate war. This is the project of European integration. The project has several elements. The most obvious is the effort to create an integrated European economy, on the premise that interdependence – the flow of people, goods and money across borders – lowers the incentive to go to war. At the same time, Europe has been demilitarized. Armed services are smaller than they were a century ago, interstate war has been proscribed under international law, and martial virtues are not glorified as they once were. Taxes that were initially levied to finance the world wars have been redirected to pay for more public services. The expansion of the welfare state after World War II buoyed public support for national governments as they proceeded with the project of integration.

Today, the project of peace-through-integration has encountered its own difficulties. We can identify five significant problems. One is a decline in long-term economic growth rates, which has made it more difficult to sustain national welfare state programs, and thereby undermined public support for political elites. Another is the economic downturn caused by the global financial crisis of 2007–8, which increased public anger even further. A third problem is the recent surge of migrants into Europe from Africa and the Middle East. A fourth is the tendency of institutions at the center of the European project to seek more influence over national policies, without due regard to the ways in which this aggravates alienation among ordinary people. A final change is the success of the project itself. Leaders and voters in 1960 knew first-hand what war was like, and this bolstered their support for integration. Today, integration can seem like a vaccine for a long-vanished disease.

This list of problems may seem overwhelming. There are some who even suggest that the project of European integration is on the verge of collapse. But this is overstatement. It would be more accurate to say that the overall policy for maintaining continental peace needs to be recalibrated, as it has been many times in the past. This may well mean a reversal of some integration policies – for example, restoring some border controls or even abandoning the common currency, the euro. But if policy reversals are effective in reducing interstate tensions and preserving continental peace, then they are justified – because it is peace, and not integration *per se*, which is the critical aim of European policy.

The sense of failure in Europe may have been aggravated because of the way in which the project of integration was presented in previous decades.

Advocates of integration sometimes presented it as a "permanent solution" to the problem of continental conflict. We like to believe that government policies will fix problems for all time, and indeed policies sometimes work better if people are persuaded that they unchangeable. In Europe, people were more likely to lay down arms and do business across borders if they believed that the project of integration could never be reversed, that it could only advance toward "ever-closer union."[6] But history suggests a different lesson about the durability of policies and institutions. Governance strategies are always unstable, either because circumstances change, or because leaders develop different opinions about the best way of managing uncertainties. From time to time, adjustments are necessary to accommodate new realities. Such adjustments are part of the normal routine of politics, not portents of collapse. The standard for judging any adjustment in Europe today is not whether it deviates from the path of integration, but whether it contributes to the extension of Europe's extraordinary long peace.

The United States has also experimented with different strategies for maintaining peace over the past three centuries, struggling with the same uncertainties and tensions that have confronted European leaders. Indeed, the United States was the product of a rebellion triggered by taxes imposed by the British Parliament to pay for war against France. But the American state did not emerge easily out of this rebellion. The treaty ending the revolution recognized the existence of thirteen states, not one. These states pulled together reluctantly. None was enthused about surrendering power to a central government. They did so to maintain a common defense against European states that still claimed territory in the new world, and to manage quarrels among the states themselves.

Indeed, the most serious challenge to American peace in the nineteenth century came from within. Tensions between northern and southern states were hard to manage. The union almost collapsed several times before the secession of eleven southern states and the outbreak of civil war in 1861. The war ended in 1865, after the death of 750,000 people, but union soldiers occupied parts of the American south for another twelve years. Internal tensions never fully dissipated afterward. In 1932, the historian Frederick Jackson Turner likened the United States to Europe. The major sections of the country were like European states, Turner said, and American politics was a "contest between sections" just as European politics was a contest between nations. "Give and take" in Washington produced laws that were like the treaties negotiated by European diplomats.[7]

Concern about the fragility of the union encouraged discipline in the management of the policy agenda of the central government: the less that Washington did, the less there was to fight about. But this feeling of fragility dissipated after World War II. Many believed that the era of sectionalism was over. In 1962 President John F. Kennedy claimed that the "sharp and emotional" divisions of the pre-World War I era had disappeared. The country, he said, now had common goals.[8] This view contributed to a growth in the number of problems taken on by the federal government between 1960 and 1980.

Unfortunately, Kennedy was guilty of wishful thinking: sectionalism had not disappeared completely. Disputes over the abuse of civil rights in southern states led again to the deployment of federal troops, a measure that President Dwight Eisenhower said was necessary to avoid "anarchy and dissolution of the union."[9] After the 1970s, the two major political parties became more clearly divided along regional lines, much as they had been before World War I. Republicans openly pursued a "southern strategy" for achieving dominance in national politics. Today, American politics is still marked by rifts between "red" and "blue" states, rural and urban regions, and white and black voters. The apparent dysfunctionality of federal government might be rooted in this reality: the collision of an expansive federal agenda with those "sharp and emotional" internal divisions that Kennedy had prematurely consigned to history. This problem is not insoluble, but it does suggest the need for an adjustment of conventional wisdom about the role of central government. Internal peace might be improved by trimming the federal policy agenda and shifting authority back to states. There is a parallel here to the challenges currently facing leaders within the European Union.

The American approach to external security also shifted over the twentieth century. In the early 1900s, most Americans were isolationists. The vastness of the Atlantic and Pacific oceans seemed to provide enough protection against attacks. Public opinion was generally hostile to the idea of a large navy and standing army. Many perceived a standing army to be a threat to liberties, and southerners were liable to regard a national army as an instrument of northern domination. Conscription, a commonplace practice in Europe at that time, was condemned as a "form of slavery" in the United States.

Two world wars, and the advent of a cold war with the Soviet Union, triggered a reappraisal of conventional wisdom about national security. By 1950, isolationism and anti-militarism had been set aside. In 1910, the country had only 126,000 military personnel on active duty, but this increased to an average of 2.7 million men between 1947 and 1975. Conscription for military service was maintained in some form for more than three decades, from 1940 to 1973. Military spending consumed about 8 percent of national income between 1947 and 1975. By contrast, the major imperial powers – Britain, France, and Germany – spent only 3 percent of national income on defense in the four decades before World War I.[10]

In fact, the decades following World War II saw an inversion of security policies in the United States and Europe. While Europe demilitarized, the United States engaged in an arms race with the Soviet Union. (Many have argued that demilitarization in Europe was possible because the United States shouldered responsibility for containing the Soviet threat.) The emphasis in the United States was on demonstrating "readiness to fight" against Soviet attacks. A 1950 national security plan recommended action around the globe to counter Soviet schemes for world domination. President

Kennedy endorsed that plan, promising to "bear any burden, meet any hardship, support any friend, [and] oppose any foe to assure the survival and the success of liberty."[11]

This aggressive policy was unsustainable. The debacle of Vietnam demonstrated the limits to what could be accomplished by hard power alone. The policy also created severe internal strains. Critics worried about the erosion of civilian control over the military, and the growth of presidential power. There was also growing resistance to the cost of the military establishment, especially as pressure for expansion of domestic programs increased in the 1960s. Added to this was youth anger over conscription, which stoked large protests on college campuses across the country. All these factors contributed to a collapse in trust in the federal government and the military in the 1970s.

This triggered another adjustment in American national security policy. The arms race with the Soviet Union continued until that country's collapse in 1991. But policymakers also became more restrained in the use of military power. Even the hawkish Reagan administration was reluctant to engage in major military action where it did not clearly serve vital interests. General Colin Powell, a senior military planner in the early 1990s, said that force should be used only when diplomatic and economic means had been exhausted. The United States also abandoned the draft in 1973, while a shift to high-tech weaponry reduced the need for manpower. The practice of relying on defense contractors with geographically dispersed operations also assured a broad political base for defense spending.

By the early 2000s, the United States appeared to have found a sustainable formula for reconciling its foreign and domestic affairs. Defense spending was reduced to 3 percent of national income – less than half of what it had been during the early Cold War – while the proportion of the population engaged in military service dropped to the lowest point since 1940. Furthermore, these were all volunteers. The federal government spent a half billion dollars a year on recruitment campaigns that celebrated military service. Trust in the military rebounded to levels not seen since the early 1960s.

But every approach to national security has its own weaknesses. In the 1990s, some experts speculated that the shift to a high-tech and all-volunteer military had revived the temptation for American policymakers to use hard power abroad. Military engagements in the 1990s contributed to the impression that it was possible to engage in "surgical" attacks that were quick, decisive, and low on casualties. This may partly explain the loosening of restraint after the terror attacks of 2001. President George W. Bush promised a Global War on Terrorism that would "rid the world of evil-doers." Pursuing a policy of "forward engagement" against terrorist networks, the United States soon found itself mired in conflicts in Iraq and Afghanistan.

The lack of clear victories in these two conflicts caused yet another recalibration of policy. The administration of President Barack Obama reduced troop levels in both countries after 2009. Obama said that the United States had "learned the hard lesson ... [that] force alone cannot impose order internationally" and promised American voters that he would "focus on nation building at home." Obama avoided significant military engagements in Libya and Syria as those two states collapsed into civil war. American public opinion broadly supported this approach, but critics said that American interventions could have reduced suffering and stopped the spread of terrorism in both countries. Some said that the United States lacked a "coherent and unified" national security policy.[12] This sense of confusion continued during the Trump administration, which combined isolationist rhetoric with belligerence against Syria and North Korea.

The Long Peace

There is ample reason to be dismayed by the way in which the Trump administration has managed these and other foreign policy challenges. Still, we can concede the difficulty of the assignment. Policymaking in the domain of national security takes place on poorly lit and constantly shifting ground. It is never entirely clear which course of action is likely to produce the intended result. Clarity and consistency of policy is desirable but not always obtainable. Frequent shifts at the edges of national strategy are more likely.

Meanwhile, it is important to recognize that the fundamentals of American national security policy are robust. The country has found a way of maintaining a powerful military apparatus without straining domestic politics. Even during President Bush's war on terrorism, the United States dedicated a smaller share of national income to defense than at any point in the Cold War. Polls consistently show that the military is the most trusted public institution in the country, with almost three-quarters of Americans expressing a high level of confidence in it. And in terms of performance, we should not take for granted the fact that national security policy has accomplished its most important goal. For three generations, it has kept the homeland free from attacks by other states.

3

The Right to Rule

Leaders of states need to be respected. More exactly, they need to be accepted as legitimate rulers of their territory. Over the centuries – and particularly over the last century – leaders of Western states have developed sophisticated ways of cultivating support for their claim to power. Some experts claim that these techniques no longer work. They see a dangerous "crisis of legitimacy" within the Western democracies. This is an exaggeration. Western governments have gone a long way to treat their people well, and people have reciprocated by maintaining solid support for the core elements of Western governance.

The problem of legitimacy has two aspects, one of which is routinely neglected by people who raise alarms about a crisis of legitimacy in the West. Usually, we focus on the attitude of ordinary people toward government. But states are also members of the system of states, and leaders worry about their standing within that system as well. In other words, legitimacy has an external as well as an internal aspect. Countries that are not accepted as members of the state system are excluded from powerful clubs like the United Nations or the International Monetary Fund. They cannot negotiate trade deals or borrow money abroad. They may even be attacked by other states, just as Afghanistan was attacked in 2001, Iraq in 2003, and Libya in 2011.

The standards that are used by the society of states to judge the legitimacy of its members have evolved over time. Until World War II, the key considerations for state recognition were whether a government had effective control of people within its borders, and whether it was itself free of control by any other state. Since World War II, however, standards have become more demanding. The society of states is less tolerant of regimes that threaten their neighbors or treat their own citizens badly. The United Nations supported military action against Afghanistan because the regime sheltered international terrorists, and against Libya because of "the gross and systematic violation of human rights" by the authorities.[1]

Can Government Do Anything Right?

The Afghan and Libyan governments suffered legitimacy crises of the external variety, with fatal consequences. But Western states never suffer this sort of crisis. They are members in good standing of the society of states. Rather, their problems relate to the apparent erosion of support for government among the people that are being governed. Internal disaffection appears to have risen to a new and possibly dangerous level.

However, we must be careful when judging whether current levels of disaffection are unusually high. Scholars sometimes point to the decay in support for public institutions that is revealed in public opinion polls taken since the 1950s. But the 1950s and 1960s might have been an especially happy time in the West. Polling did not really get started until the early 1950s, so we cannot compare to earlier years. Furthermore, we tend to look at history through rose-colored glasses. We forget the uprisings, strikes, protests, and riots that were commonplace in Western countries before World War II. Even in the supposedly upbeat '50s and '60s, Western democracies were afflicted by industrial strikes as well as protests over civil rights, the Vietnam war, and the nuclear arms race. (There were 3,700 major work stoppages in the United States in 1950–9, compared to just 200 in 2000–9.)

Moreover, some Western states were still imperial powers at that time. People in Kenya, Algeria, Angola, and the Congo were in open rebellion against their European rulers.

We should abandon the notion that there was ever a halcyon era in which people were at peace with their governments. Nobody likes to be governed. The intensity of disaffection may vary, and there may be moments of relative calm, but these moments are transitory. The danger that public opinion will turn sour, and that discontent will spark protests or disrespect for the law, never dissipates entirely.

Over the last two centuries, the Western leaders have improved methods for containing such discontent. They have improved their police forces and adopted laws that dictate when and where protests are allowed. But these hard methods of containing discontent have limits. Leaders have also experimented with techniques that are aimed at cultivating positive support for government. These techniques are of two types: power-preserving and power-limiting.

Power-preserving techniques are aimed at building support without compromising the power of the central executive. The classical version of this technique plays on the public's fear of disorder and its desire for physical safety. In the sixteenth century, the jurist Jean Bodin justified the absolute power of French kings as a bulwark against "licentious anarchy, which is worse than the harshest tyranny in the world."[2] A few years later, the English philosopher Thomas Hobbes defended absolutism as the only way of preventing civil war and the "ruin of mankind."[3] Bodin and Hobbes had survived civil wars and knew what anarchy and ruin looked like. So did many of their compatriots, who were prepared to tolerate autocratic government if it produced peace and order.

Another power-preserving technique is the appeal to national identity and pride. Leaders promote the idea that the governed population constitutes one people or nation with a common culture and destiny, and they present the state as the main instrument by which the nation preserves its culture and pursues its destiny. The line between the state and the governed population is blurred, so that states are transformed into nation-states. Nationalistic appeals were popular in the nineteenth century. Leaders tried to build a sense of common identity and pride within their populations by standardizing education, celebrating patriotism, and launching great national projects. Often, those projects involved wars against other states as well as the construction of empires. Nationalism fit with the militaristic ethos of the nineteenth and early twentieth centuries. Extreme nationalism bred intolerance of minorities as well. It also had unintended consequences, as minorities demanded the right to self-determination on the grounds of their own distinctiveness as a people.

Nationalistic appeals were discredited, but not entirely abandoned, after World War II. Indeed, all developed countries still look for ways to cultivate national unity – for example, through culture and sport – and, in particular, to build loyalty among recent immigrants. In 2001, the administration of George W. Bush generated support for its policies by appealing to the providential role of the American people as promoters of liberty around the globe. The current Chinese government justifies itself as an instrument for the restoration of the nation's honor and its place at the center of Asian civilization. In the early 2000s in the United Kingdom, the government of Prime Minister Gordon Brown began a campaign to promote "Britishness," arguing that the erosion of a common identity had undermined internal order and respect for the law.

The third power-preserving technique of legitimation is enrichment of citizens. Loyalty to the state is purchased in one way or another. Leaders can provide more benefits and services to citizens, just as Western governments did in the aftermath of World War II. Or they may try to stimulate the growth of the economy, hoping that people will be satisfied by higher incomes obtained in the private sector. It is likely that popular support for Western governments in the two decades following World War II was bolstered not just by the expansion of the welfare state, but also by high growth following two decades of depression and war. Today, the Chinese government also relies on rapid growth to maintain its popularity with the Chinese people. But the technique of enrichment has perils as well. The influence that governments have over the economy is greater than it was a century ago, but it is far from perfect: by relying heavily on growth as the foundation for legitimacy, leaders leave themselves vulnerable to the vagaries of the market-place. And rapid growth can be a mixed blessing. A boom in one part of the country can cause massive internal migration – as in China today, and in the United States in the last century – and this collision of people may trigger unrest. Heightened inequality can also cause trouble, even when poorer citizens are better off than before.

An important distinction between Western democracies and autocratic states like China is that the former have developed a broader range of techniques for maintaining internal legitimacy. This is another significant accomplishment of Western governments. We can classify these additional tools as power-limiting techniques. In a variety of ways, they limit the discretion of the powerful monarch once celebrated by Bodin and Hobbes.

The most radical power-limiting technique is the complete surrender of authority over people. Britain provides the best example of this approach. In 1900, the British Parliament asserted the right to rule over 400 million subjects, of whom only forty million lived in the British Isles. British troops were often used to suppress colonial protests and rebellions in the early twentieth century. This was a genuine crisis of legitimacy that was resolved when British leaders relinquished their power over nine-tenths of the empire's population. More broadly, decolonization resulted in the creation of over 100 new states after World War II. It has improved legitimacy by reducing the distance between rulers and the ruled.

There are less radical power-limiting techniques. One is federalization: the surrender of power by central executives to regional governments within the state. The United States was the earliest model of an extensive federal state, but the British Empire spawned many others, including Canada, Australia, India, and Nigeria. Paradoxically, British leaders have struggled with the concept of federalization at home. For a long time, British experts viewed it as an evil that should be tolerated only when absolutely necessary in large and diverse countries like the United States or India. The respected jurist A.V. Dicey insisted that federalization sapped the strength of the state. "Federal government," Dicey claimed, "means weak government."[4] In recent decades, resistance to federalism within the United Kingdom has diminished. Power has been devolved from the British Parliament to new governing bodies for Scotland, Wales, and Northern Ireland. But there is still confusion about the best way of devolving power within England, and also about the proper scope of central authority within this newly federalized system.

A third power-limiting technique is the establishment of the rule of law, which obliges central executives to give up power to assemblies (that is, parliaments or congresses) and courts. Executive prerogatives – the freedom of executives to act autonomously – are largely or wholly eliminated. Assemblies acquire the power to guide executive action by passing laws, while independent courts acquire the right to review executive actions to determine whether they conform to those laws.

A fourth power-limiting technique is the constitutional entrenchment of individual rights. These constitutional "bills of rights" identify the range of actions that executives and assemblies are prohibited from taking, such as restricting freedom of speech, imprisoning people without trial, or treating people differently because of their race or religion. Since World War II, bills of rights are more likely to impose positive obligations on government as well. For example, they may establish a duty to provide education, healthcare, or a basic level of income. Initially regarded as forms of governmental largesse, these services and benefits are now seen as entitlements. In this sense, they are checks on state power: they impose encumbrances on state resources and limit the maneuvering room of leaders.

A fifth power-limiting technique is the extension of the elective principle, which says that important officers within the state should be elected for a limited term by some part of the general population. There are debates about which officers should be elected, and who should vote in elections. In most of the advanced democracies, however, the minimal expectation is that assemblies will be composed mainly of people who are selected through elections in which almost all adult citizens vote.

Can Government Do Anything Right?

Leaders in Western countries have applied all these power-limiting techniques with the aim of cultivating public support for government. The result has been the construction in each country of a complex constitutional and legal architecture that channels and constrains the exercise of executive power. Sometimes we talk about this architecture as though it has been with us for a very long time. This is a bit of sleight of hand. We emphasize the venerable history of our governing institutions to discourage tinkering with constitutional and legal arrangements that we value highly. In fact, though, we tinker with this architecture all the time, and some of its features are quite new.

For example, consider the elective principle. The practice of allowing almost every adult to vote is not that old. There are millions of people living in the Western world who were born before the advent of this practice. Most Western states did not allow women to vote until World War I; in France, this change did not happen until 1945. Property restrictions were not eliminated completely in Britain until 1928. In the American south, most African Americans were unable to vote until the 1960s.[5] Opinions about the counting of votes have also changed, with a shift toward proportional representation systems in many countries. And there are ongoing debates about which offices should be directly elected. Presidents of the United States are still not directly elected, although many believe that they should be. There is movement away from electing judges in the United States, but movement toward the election of police chiefs in the United Kingdom. Canadians still maintain an unelected upper legislative chamber, while Britons continue to wrestle over the presence of hereditary peers in their House of Lords.

The rule of law is another concept that has proved to be malleable in practice. The principle says that executives must be guided by laws drafted by assemblies, but in the early twentieth century, overwhelmed assemblies returned some law-making powers back to the executive. The principle also says that courts should decide whether executives are complying with the law. However, courts have gone back and forth on how aggressively they should exercise such oversight. After the 1970s, courts and assemblies were generally tougher on executives. Courts became more critical of executive decision-making, and assemblies passed more laws dictating precisely how executives should do their work, for example by mandating more openness and public consultation. Assemblies also established many independent "watchdog" agencies in the latter part of the twentieth century – to stand up for privacy or the environment, scrutinize spending, prevent corruption, and so on. In some countries, this group of independent monitors is said to constitute an entirely new branch of government.

There has been similar experimentation with the ideas of federalization and entrenchment of rights. As we have noted, British policymakers still struggle to define the appropriate roles of parliament and regional governments, while American policymakers still argue about the division of responsibilities between the federal and state governments. In many countries, courts and assemblies also debate over the range of protected rights. Much of the law here is also new. The right to privacy has only been acknowledged in law since the 1960s, and its exact boundaries are still uncertain. The right to fair treatment by government is also more expansive than it was in the 1960s. The right to protection against discrimination based on sexual orientation is still being consolidated in some places. Increasingly, many Americans acknowledge a right to healthcare, although they disagree about how government should honor that right.

The overall trend in Western countries in the twentieth century has been toward the increased use of power-limiting techniques for building public support for government. Leaders have cultivated legitimacy by checking and diffusing power. Many of these constitutional and legal reforms are also justified as ways of promoting fundamental human rights, so leaders see an opportunity to advance an important normative project – that is, to advance the public welfare – while also bolstering support for the state. Of course, better protection of human rights also bolsters the external legitimacy of states as well.

However, there are conservatives who complain that Western countries have developed an unhealthy fixation on power-limiting techniques. They have three main concerns. The first is whether governments have the resources to continue providing those services and benefits that have been transformed into entitlements over the last sixty years. We will consider this problem in more detail in Chapter 5. The second is whether there really is a link between power-limiting measures and improved trust. For example, we like to believe that people will tolerate laws if they have been given the right to vote for lawmakers, but the evidence is hardly definitive.

The third conservative complaint is that the weakening of executive authority may actually undermine legitimacy, for example by crippling the capacity of leaders to act decisively in the face of threats to national security. The administration of President George W. Bush advanced this criticism even before the terror attacks of September 11, 2001. Defense Secretary Donald Rumsfeld compared American government to Gulliver tied down by the Lilliputians, describing it as a body rendered impotent by a dense web of checks and restrictions. The Bush administration used the 9/11 attacks as a pretext for cutting through some of these controls. The United States entered a de facto state of emergency, in which legal constraints were loosened as part of a broader effort to "keep America safe." The administration justified its power by playing on fear and promising safety, just as Bodin and Hobbes had recommended. This approach worked for a short time: trust in government soared to heights not seen since the 1960s. But fear eventually diminished and trust in government slumped again.

Conservatives have made similar complaints about the enfeeblement of government since the global financial crisis of 2007–8. The distinguished scholar Francis Fukuyama has claimed that the American system is "in decay" because of the country's obsession with the fragmentation of political authority. He has called for a rollback

46

of some of the power-limiting reforms of the last four decades, arguing that a stronger executive will perform key functions more effectively, thus restoring trust in government.[6] Some populist movements offer a similar critique of modern government. They put their faith in strong leaders who have the capacity to amass power and break through gridlock. In the United States, voters said that they supported presidential candidate Donald Trump because he was "tough" and seemed likely to "get things done."[7] Like populist leaders in other countries, Trump shifted toward power-preserving techniques of legitimation, playing on nationalist sentiments and feelings of insecurity.

Leaders in autocratic countries like China have gone even further in their criticism of power-limiting techniques, arguing that recent history has exposed the fundamental weaknesses of Western liberal democracy. Chinese leaders seem to retain public support without relying extensively on the rule of law, democracy, or entrenched human rights. Surveys suggest that an overwhelming majority of Chinese people – indeed, a much larger share of the population than in most advanced democracies – are satisfied with their country's direction.[8] But we should not rush to judgment about the superiority of the Chinese approach. One observer warns that the

Chinese system "reposes unsteadily on a two-legged stool" of rapid growth and nationalism.[9]

In fact, no country has found a permanent solution to the problem of maintaining public support for government. Western leaders, like Chinese leaders, experiment constantly with different techniques for building legitimacy, fully conscious that every technique has advantages and disadvantages. The current Western approach may have its flaws, but we should not take this observation too far. Polls show dissatisfaction with the recent performance of major institutions, but they also reveal a deep commitment to basic principles like the rule of law and self-governance. The debate in the West is about the application and balancing of techniques, not about fundamentals.

People in the West agree on fundamentals because they appreciate the immense gains for human welfare achieved through the deployment of power-limiting techniques. Overall, the last century has seen remarkable progress on human rights in most developed countries. This is another fact that should be remembered when judging the overall performance of our governments. Never before have people had more influence over their leaders, more protection against arbitrary governmental action, and more room for self-expression. Through the extension of government services, people are better educated, longer-lived, and better protected against the distress that was once associated with old age, disability or illness. Of course, developed countries can always strive to do better. But we are a long way from the world of 1900, when the average person in countries like the United Kingdom or the United States had only a few years of primary education, a life expectancy at birth of about fifty years, little protection against discrimination and extreme poverty, and no significant role in the selection of rulers. Most people in the West in 1900 were mere subjects. Today they are citizens.

4

Taming the Economy

During the 2016 US presidential race, pollsters asked Americans what issue would be foremost on their minds as they cast their votes. The most common answer was the economy. Most people agreed that the economy had performed badly and that its prospects were poor. Good jobs were scarce and inequality was rising. Voters were also asked which candidate, Trump or Clinton, would be better at managing the economy. There was no clear favorite. People were unsure about whether the economy would be better off with more government intervention or less, and whether the policy of open borders helped the economy or hurt it. Voters in other countries are often asked similar questions and give similar answers. This sense of confusion about the economy – what has gone wrong with it, and how to fix it – contributes powerfully to dissatisfaction with government in the Western democracies.

The problems with many Western economies are real, although not entirely new. Fortunately, we have an invention that can help us deal with these problems. It is probably one of the most important inventions of the twentieth century, although we have taken it for granted, and recently toyed with abandoning it. This invention is the concept of the economy itself: a bounded system that can be measured and managed in the public interest.

Before the 1930s, nobody talked about "the economy."[1] Certainly, leaders recognized the major spheres of economic activity: agriculture, manufacturing, trade and commerce, and banking and finance. They knew that these spheres were connected and that together they produced a condition that was typically described as national prosperity or national wealth. But there was no agreement on how the parts fit together to form a single system. Nor was there agreement – in an age in which money, commodities and people flowed easily between countries – that the boundaries of that system coincided with national borders. The statistical capacities of government were crude. Data that we take for granted today – the unemployment rate, the interest rate, the inflation rate – was unavailable. There was no standard measure of national prosperity and its change from year to year. It was commonplace to compare economic conditions – "the state of trade" – to the weather. This was at a time when the capacity to map and forecast weather patterns was primitive. Clearly there were seasonal weather patterns, but from day to day it was very changeable, and often dangerously so. Devastating storms often blew up without warning. Similarly, there appeared to be a broad rhythm to economic affairs – a cycle of good times and hard times – but the risk of a sudden crash or slump was ever-present, and there was no way to see it coming.

For governments, this was an awkward situation. It was part of the general problem of lacking mastery over circumstances. Leaders understood the importance of national prosperity. An increase in wealth meant more tax revenue to pay for national defense, internal policing, and the conciliation of powerful factions. Conversely, hard times meant an increase in strikes, riots and rebellions. But no one really knew how to improve prosperity and avoid slumps. Ignorance about the dynamics of trade and commerce made it difficult to predict the effect of government actions. And in any case, governments had limited capacity to act. Leaders did not have the policy tools that we take for granted today. The US government did not have a unified budget until the 1920s, which made "fiscal policy" hard to imagine. Neither the US nor British governments had direct control over their central banks, which made "monetary policy" hard to imagine. The agencies charged with regulating key industries were small and powerless.

In addition to ignorance and administrative incapacity, two other factors constrained government action relating to industry, trade and finance. One was the structure of domestic politics. Before the 1920s, most adults could not vote, and power lay heavily in the hands of industrialists, financiers and landowners. The other factor was the structure of international politics. In an era in which interstate war was a real possibility, it was important to have a strong industrial base within national borders to support militarization. But industrial expansion often depended on access to lenders, customers, and raw materials in other countries. This created a vulnerability: prosperity and security hinged on the whims of foreign leaders regarding access to markets.

The governance strategies of Western countries before the 1930s were tailored to accommodate these constraints. Within national borders, leaders pursued a policy of laissez faire. Industrialists were permitted to build large enterprises without hindrance by government regulation or strong labor unions. Tariffs on imported manufactures provided protection against foreign competition. A commitment to the gold standard meant that creditors were protected during slumps, because governments could not rescue lenders by diluting the value of the currency. Western leaders often used force to guarantee access to foreign markets. European states constructed empires, while the United States and other nations used military threats to open markets in Asia and Latin America.

This overall strategy for promoting national prosperity became untenable after World War I. Colonial rebellions and the rhetoric of national self-determination made it difficult for Western states to maintain market access by force. Meanwhile, laissez faire created strains at home. Industrialization was accompanied by dramatic increases in economic inequality. Critics complained that industrialists and financiers had corrupted nascent democratic institutions, and that countries like the United States and the United Kingdom had become plutoc-racies – that is, systems of rule by the rich and for the rich. The boom-and-bust cycle persisted as well. The United States suffered through a half

dozen panics and slumps between 1890 and the
Great Crash of 1929. This produced severe social
and political instability. Extremist movements –
anarchism, communism, fascism – grew in strength
across the West.

These decades of instability produced important
changes in the governance strategies of Western
countries. Some of these changes put more power in
the hands of ordinary people. In the United States, for
example, the right to vote was extended, the administration of elections was improved, US senators were
directly elected for the first time, the primary system
of nominations was introduced, and legal restrictions
on campaign financing were adopted. All of this was
done with the aim of breaking the economic and
political power of industrialists and financiers.

Accompanying these political reforms were
improvements in economic knowledge and governmental capacity to influence economic activity.
These two developments were closely linked.
Between the 1910s and 1930s, governments
enhanced their ability to collect statistics about
economic activity. At the same time, economists
developed new ways of defining and measuring
"national accounts" and "national income."
Experts talked more confidently about the contours
of the "national economic system" and eventually

about the "national economy." Theories about the likely effect of different government interventions became more sophisticated. More experts worked in government agencies that were responsible for developing overall economic plans, crafting budgets, setting policies on money and credit, and regulating major industries.

In the United States, this transformation in governmental capabilities accelerated with the election of Franklin D. Roosevelt in 1932 and was largely completed during the post-war presidency of Harry Truman. Roosevelt began his presidency without the most basic information about economic conditions, such as the number of people unemployed in the United States. His administration had to jury-rig mechanisms for dispensing aid, reviving industry and creating jobs. Truman, by contrast, was supported by a new Council of Economic Advisers, an improved Budget Bureau and central bank, and a phalanx of agencies specializing in the distribution of aid and economic regulation. By law, Truman was required to publish an annual report assessing the state of the economy and outlining his plans for promoting "maximum employment, production and purchasing power."

These developments were not unique to the United States. All Western countries went through a similar transformation. By the early 1950s, the concept of the economy was part of everyday conversation. Everyone understood that the economy could be managed, and that responsibility for managing it lay mainly with central government. Executives like the US president were given the bureaucratic tools needed to fulfill this responsibility, while citizens acquired the political tools needed to hold executives accountable. At the same time, universities trained more experts and refined knowledge about how the economy worked. All of this constituted a sophisticated scheme for achieving mastery over economic affairs and assuring that the economy was managed in the public interest.

Economies were also shaped so that they were easier to manage. Conceptually, the boundaries of every economy were defined to be the same as the borders of a state. Each country had its own economy, which interacted with other economies but could be managed as a stand-alone system. Policies adopted after World War II defined the boundaries between economies more clearly. The agreement establishing the International Monetary Fund in 1944 allowed states to limit the flow of capital across national borders. Governments backed away from the gold standard, giving themselves more discretion to adjust the value of their currency during booms and slumps. At roughly the same time, Western countries adopted a new regime for managing access to overseas markets, one which relied less heavily on the use of force. Known as the General Agreement on Tariffs and Trade (GATT), the regime reduced the risk that countries would renege on promises regarding market access. In 1993, GATT was transformed into the World Trade Organization (WTO).

The post-war economic boom caused many leaders and experts to become over-confident about their capacity to control economic conditions. There was a sense that economies had been tamed for good, and that all that remained were "technical questions" about the best way of promoting growth.[2] In the mid-1960s, experts explained how government policies could be adjusted to "fine-tune" the economy.[3] But this confidence was shattered over the next fifteen years, provoking further changes in the governance strategies of Western states.

Policymakers in the 1950s and 1960s had under-estimated the plasticity of markets. The institutions and laws that are set up to regulate the economy are necessarily rigid. But the economy itself is metamorphic: its shape changes constantly, in ways that undermine the effectiveness of those institutions and laws. Businesses and households learn how to anticipate and evade government actions, so that those actions no longer yield the same results. Other factors – such as the advent of new technologies, the rise of foreign competitors, or disruption of access to key resources – also induce fundamental changes in the structure of the economy, so that institutions and laws quickly become outmoded. Such considerations were also at play in the late 1960s and 1970s.

Shifts in domestic and international politics were also important in driving policy change. At home, in the 1970s, voters became angry about slow growth and high inflation. Meanwhile businesses were frustrated by declining profitability, and eager to exploit opportunities in rising Asian economies. Advances in information and transportation technologies made it easier for businesses to send manufacturing functions abroad and coordinate cross-border production chains. Governments that were normally leery about increasing dependence on foreign markets were reassured by the long post-war peace. Many experts argued that more international trade and finance would consolidate that peace, because countries with economic links were unlikely to fight each other.

By the late 1980s, leading Western countries had made important shifts in their strategies for managing the economy. Internally, governments reduced their role in guiding economic activity. Regulations were rescinded and government-owned businesses were returned to private ownership. Diplomatic efforts to reduce tariffs and other barriers to trade were intensified. Countries also removed limits on the flow of capital across national borders. The result, by the end of the century, was a massive jump in the volume of cross-border trade and investment. The structure of advanced economies was dramatically altered, as manufacturing declined and finance grew in economic importance and political clout.

Many people thought that the world was reverting to conditions like those before World War I. Indeed, there were similarities. Some countries were experiencing levels of trade and cross-border investment not seen since the end of the nineteenth century. Of course, the concept of the national economy was unknown in 1900, and many experts said that it was becoming obsolete in the 1990s. They claimed that national economies had been merged into a single, global economy. National governments were said to have little power in this second age of globalization. States, Kenichi Ohmae wrote in 1995, had "lost their role as meaningful units of participation in the global economy of today's borderless world."[4] The political scientist Susan

Strange suggested that national leaders had "lost the authority over national societies and economies that they used to have."[5]

Many experts were unfazed by the re-emergence of a global economy. On the contrary, they celebrated its virtues. There was a revival of the sort of hubris that had typified the 1960s. This was encouraged by a burst in growth in the late 1990s. Experts ignored evidence that people were becoming angry about increasing inequality, arguing that even the poorest were better off than they had been before. "A rising tide," it was said, "lifts all boats." Similarly, experts dismissed signs that the old pattern of boom and bust had returned. There were crises in Mexico, Thailand, Russia, and Argentina, but these were usually dismissed as problems on the periphery of the global economy. Of course, the global financial crisis of 2007–8 shattered this self-confidence. The experts were proved wrong. They had underestimated the political dangers of rising inequality and overestimated the "self-stabilizing" properties of the globalized economy.[6]

Fortunately, experts were also wrong in a second sense. Although global flows of trade and finance had undoubtedly surged after the 1980s, the concept of the national economy had not been made obsolete. The administrative capacity that was necessary to formulate and execute economic policy was still available, even if it was not used as aggressively as it had been in the 1950s and 1960s. The idea that national leaders were responsible for managing the economy also persisted. Even Ronald Reagan, who wanted to reduce government control of the market system, could not liberate himself from responsibility for the performance of that system. The political mechanisms that allowed voters to enforce that responsibility, which had been expanded and improved in the first era of globalization, were still operative.

The result has been a revival of the concept of the national economy since the global financial crisis. Western governments responded quickly to the crisis, using all the tools at their disposal to avoid a complete economic collapse. Failing banks were rescued, major businesses were nationalized, and consumer demand was propped up by fiscal and monetary stimulus. Governments worked with each other to coordinate their policies and avoid destructive tariff and currency wars. "The system worked," the political scientist Daniel Drezner has argued. Policymakers responded to the crisis "in an effective and nimble fashion."[7] This seems a little too generous: after all, the system would have done better if it had avoided crisis in the first place.

Still, quick interventions by national governments avoided a reprise of the chaos of the 1930s. This was only possible because leaders had the administrative capacity and political responsibility to protect their national economies.

Strategies for managing national economies have continued to evolve in the decade since the financial crisis, driven by the refusal of voters to continue with the economic formulas that were applied in the thirty years preceding the crisis. Much of the rhetoric of the last decade is drawn from the early 1900s. We are once again debating whether Western government has become a system of "rule for the rich, by the rich." When Occupy Wall Street challenged the power of the "one percent" it was borrowing a phrase introduced a century ago. A critical difference, however, is that the channels for expression of public discontent are better than they were before World War I. Reformers today do not have to fight for the franchise. As a result, leaders are more responsive to public discontent.

It is still unclear how economic policies will be adjusted in response to this discontent, but one effect will likely be a retreat from the full-scale liberalization of the late twentieth century. Western leaders are experimenting with tighter regulation and asking whether there should be limits to the uninhibited flow of trade and finance across borders. We are unlikely to see a wholesale reversal of the developments of the last thirty years, but leaders are clearly drawing bolder lines of demarcation around their national economies.

Indeed, leaders also have their own reasons for marking the boundaries between national economies more clearly. The international environment has altered over the last quarter century. In the early 1990s, the Cold War had just ended, and it appeared that Russia might become a friend of the West. China also seemed to be moving toward the Western model of governance, and was still a relatively small economy. This was the moment at which Francis Fukuyama famously celebrated the "unabashed victory of economic and political liberalism."[8] In those circumstances, Western leaders did not see much risk associated with increased interdependence. Today, though, the world has changed. China and Russia no longer seem like friendly powers, and the Chinese economy is the biggest in the world by some measures.[9] Interdependence now poses larger risks. Western leaders worry about the loss of manufacturing capacities that are critical to national security, about the sharing of defense-related technologies, and about corporate takeovers by businesses that are controlled by foreign governments.

As we can see, the work of achieving mastery over economic affairs is not easy. The pursuit of mastery always runs up against the complexity and plasticity of the modern economy. "Economic activity," one expert has observed, "is like quicksilver."[10] Having said this, we should not underestimate the accomplishments of the last century. Leaders in Western countries know much more about the workings of their national economies than they did a century ago. Their ability to monitor the flow of production, commerce, and finance is vastly improved. Leaders also have a broader range of tools for defining the boundaries of the economy and shaping behavior within it. And they are also burdened with the duty to use those tools. Privately, leaders might want to slough off their responsibility for managing the economy, but pollsters and voters will not let them get away with it.

Most countries in the world do not have these advantages. In those countries, most people work in the "informal" or "grey" sector, beyond the sight of government agencies. Leaders lack good information about the patterns of trade and finance within the borders of their territory, and policy tools to shape that activity. There are severe problems of economic inequality and instability in those countries as well, but there is little that can be done to address those problems. As a practical matter, the national economy is unknown and ungovernable territory. But this is not so in the advanced democracies.

5

The Battle of the Bulge

In 2014 two editors of *The Economist*, John Micklethwait and Adrian Wooldridge, published a grim assessment of government in the Western world. They said that recent history had revealed a potentially fatal flaw in democratic government: its tendency to cause an inexorable expansion of the state. Democracy, it was alleged, had become "sloppy and self-indulgent." Voters dodged difficult choices and overloaded their governments with obligations. As a result, the typical Western state is "bloated and overwhelmed ... a gigantic mess [that is] supersized by ambition and pulled hither and thither by conflicting aims."[1]

The argument presented by Micklethwait and Wooldridge is not new. It is known as the "overload thesis," and it was first advanced to explain the economic and political malaise that afflicted many advanced democracies in the 1970s. You might be dismayed to see the same thesis advanced today: it might seem that Western countries have learned nothing over forty years. But this is not the case. In fact, the overload thesis does not fit the facts as readily as it did forty years ago. Politicians and voters in the West have learned how to govern themselves more carefully. They have made difficult decisions and restrained their demands on government.

The average person living today has no memory of the tumultuous 1970s. The mood was not much different than it is today. The Western world was weighed down by a sense of failure and drift. James Reston, a columnist for the *New York Times*, wrote in 1975: "It is hard to travel in Europe these days, or even to live in Washington, without recognizing that liberal democracy is in serious trouble in the world. The leaders of the Free World seem to be overwhelmed by the complexities of modern life, baffled by the demands of special-interest groups, and inclined toward autocratic methods in handling their dilemmas."[2]

In 1974, the Trilateral Commission – a newly formed group of concerned businessmen and intellectuals – commissioned a study to determine what had gone wrong in the West. The report that was issued the following year predicted a "bleak future for democratic government."[3] The West German chancellor Willy Brandt thought that all of Western Europe might slide into dictatorship by the end of the century. The British historian Arnold Toynbee thought that democracy might give way to "ruthless authoritarian government."[4]

Two ideas contributed to the sense of malaise. The first was the belief that Western governments had lost control of events. A feeling of economic and social breakdown was pervasive. The post-war economic boom had ended and national inflation rates were reaching heights rarely experienced in peacetime. Serious crime, urban rioting, and incidents of terrorism were on the increase. In some countries, the number of major strikes surged to levels not seen in decades.

Another idea was that Western governments had lost control *of themselves*: that they were no longer able to act in a steady and disciplined way. For example, some economists argued that inflation was aggravated by the erratic way in which politicians wielded control over monetary policy. This was supposed to be a tool for fine-tuning the economy. But leaders were not acting like technicians, carefully adjusting the dial on interest rates to assure price stability. Instead, they spun the dial recklessly, seeking to boost the economy before elections, and then to calm it down afterward. Businesses and households had no clear idea of what governments might do in the future.

This lack of self-discipline also seemed to be evident in the domain of fiscal policy. This was supposed to be another tool for fine-tuning the economy: governments would run deficits to prime the pump during hard times, but compensate with surpluses during good times. But politicians did not seem to behave this way. They were eager to prime the pump, especially before elections, but slow to pay down debts later. The result, by the mid-1970s, was an unprecedented pattern of peacetime deficit spending and mounting public debt.

There was more evidence of indiscipline. Conservatives pointed to the growth of government regulation and bureaucracy, regardless of which political party was in charge. In the United States, Democratic president Lyndon Johnson (1963–8) improved pensions and health insurance for the aged, increased aid for cities and schools, and announced a broad "war on poverty." Republican president Richard Nixon (1969–74) established the Environmental Protection Agency, the Occupational Safety and Health Administration, and the Consumer Product Safety Commission, approved the Endangered Species Act, and expanded rules against discrimination in the workplace. Federal non-defense spending (as a share of GDP) increased by 90 percent between 1960 and 1975, while civilian employment increased by 20 percent. Not only was government bureaucracy larger in most Western countries, it also appeared to be less effective. There was mounting evidence that government programs were wasting resources and failing to achieve objectives.

By the late 1970s many scholars were writing about a "crisis of governability" in the West. Conservatives offered two explanations of what had gone wrong. Some, adopting the argument of the Trilateral Commission report, tied the crisis to the expansion of voting rights and the reduction of other barriers to public participation in governmental decision-making. There had been a broad "democratic surge" in the 1960s and early 1970s which resulted in more calls for government services, and a simultaneous decline in deference to public institutions. Norms of self-restraint had decayed. There was an "excess of democracy," the authors of the report concluded. Leaders were overloaded by the public's demands.

Conservative economists offered a somewhat different interpretation. They argued that all the players in the great game of democratic politics

– citizens, interest groups, politicians, and bureau-crats – should be regarded as actors who seek only to advance their own material interests. For citizens, this means pressuring politicians to provide more benefits. For politicians, it means appeasing voters in order to stay in office. For bureaucrats, it means manipulating politicians to obtain bigger budgets than are necessary to provide services. All players follow their selfish proclivities, but the rules of the game are poorly designed, so that the outcome is myopic decision-making and inexorable growth in the size of government.

Both explanations struck at the core of Western democracy. The complaint was not merely that passing circumstances had caused a momentary derangement in government. Rather, there appeared to be something intrinsic to the design of democratic systems that would generate bad outcomes in perpetuity. In 2014, Micklethwait and Wooldridge suggested there might be an "iron law of modern politics" that government must go on getting bigger.[5] The fact that this idea could still be advanced after four decades suggests that there must be something to the argument that there is some *inherent* flaw in democracy.

But the track record of Western governments over the last four decades is not nearly so grim as Micklethwait and Woolridge (and others) have suggested. In fact, Western governments did learn from the experience of the 1970s. Over the following decades, they altered their approach to governing. The design of Western democracies changed. The problems of the 1970s did not disappear, but the track record of Western governments in managing those problems is better than we might appreciate.

Consider the problem of inflation. In the 1970s, many people thought that runaway inflation was the most powerful example of governmental indiscipline, and much more serious than the emerging pattern of deficit spending. In the United States, an overwhelming majority of voters said that inflation was their top concern. Experts warned that inflation had caused the death of democracy in Germany in the 1920s. Some questioned whether Western leaders would ever muster the courage to take the painful decisions necessary to stop it. Clearly, though, they did. Among advanced economies, the inflation rate dropped from about 9 percent at the start of the 1980s to about 2 percent by the end of the 1990s. Inflation has not been a serious problem in major Western democracies for almost three decades.

This was accomplished thanks to a growing intolerance of high inflation on the part of voters and politicians, and an eventual shift in policies and institutions. In the United States and the United Kingdom, conservative leaders took steps to undermine the bargaining power of unions, which eased upward pressure on wages. Trade liberalization, and easier access to inexpensive imports, put downward pressure on prices. More importantly, however, politicians surrendered control over monetary policy. Central banks were given the independence needed to make the hard decisions on inflation control. In the United States, Federal Reserve chairman Alan Greenspan became the archetype of the powerful and autonomous central banker. The Bank of England was granted similar independence in 1997, and so was the European Central Bank when it was established in 1998. Scholars have described central bankers as a "modern embodiment of the Platonic guardian," effectively operating as a fourth branch of government, with the mandate to maintain price stability.[6]

Governments tried to create guardians of fiscal policy as well. Experts suggested that one way of achieving budget discipline was to increase the power of finance ministers, so that they could contain the pressure for increased spending coming from other parts of government. In the United Kingdom this was known as "Treasury power." It was a fact of life after the 1980s. In 2010, the British government also set up an independent watchdog, the Office of Budget Responsibility, to check the accuracy of fiscal plans. The government of Prime Minister Tony Blair adopted another control device as well: a "fiscal policy code" that required a balanced budget over the economic cycle.

The code was a kind of "fiscal rule." This was an invention that became popular around the world in the post-1970s era. A fiscal rule is a legal constraint that requires budget balance, or prohibits deficits or debts beyond a certain point. It serves as a straight-jacket for wayward governments. The United States came close to adopting a constitutional prohibition on budget deficits at the federal level in the late 1970s and early 1980s.[7] While a constitutional amendment was never achieved, the US Congress did adopt a balanced budget statute in 1985, which continued in operation with modifications until 2002. In Europe, the Maastricht Treaty of 1992 set deficit and debt limits for governments that were adopting the euro, while the 1997 Stability and Growth Pact established mechanisms for enforcing the Maastricht limits. Fiscal rules for the euro countries were toughened in the wake of the global financial crisis. Many advanced economies outside Europe also experimented with fiscal rules.

Critics of fiscal rules point out that politicians have a checkered record in complying with them. American and European politicians found loopholes or simply ignored the rules when economic conditions deteriorated. But this does not mean that fiscal rules were ineffective. The fact that they were being debated and adopted is evidence that norms about budgetary discipline were being restored. Leaders also paid a political price when the rules were evaded or suspended. The battle to restore fiscal discipline was never won cleanly, but Western governments made substantial progress. In 1995, central government debt in the advanced economies averaged about 55 percent of GDP. By 2007, this had been reduced to about 45 percent. Certainly, the debt burden grew as governments responded to the global financial crisis, but that was caused by the need to manage a massive market failure, not by some problem of indiscipline that was intrinsic to democracy.

The United States was among the countries that had a reasonable track record of restoring fiscal discipline after the 1970s. It is important to emphasize this, given the ongoing tradition of condemning out-of-control spending in Washington. In the 1950s, federal spending was equal to about 17 percent of GDP. It crept up to 22 percent of

GDP by the mid-1980s, but declined after the early 1990s. The average for the decade preceding the financial crisis was 18.6 percent. Despite the growth of programs like Social Security, Medicare, and Medicaid, and wars in Iraq and Afghanistan, spending was not much higher than it had been a half century earlier. Federal debt held by the public declined from 48 percent of GDP in the early 1990s to 35 percent in 2007, roughly where it had been in 1965. Of course, the financial crisis upended fiscal policy in the United States, just as it did in Europe. But this does not diminish the track record in reasserting control over fiscal policy during the preceding two decades.

Conservative intellectuals in the 1970s also had a harsh view of bureaucrats. The British television comedy *Yes Minister*, originally broadcast between 1980 and 1984, conveyed that view to a general audience. The co-author of the series, Sir Antony Jay, drew on a scholarly literature that depicted public servants as schemers who dupe their masters to gain larger budgets and lavish perquisites. They were called "budget-maximizing bureaucrats." Their behavior, it was alleged, contributed to an ever-expanding and wasteful public sector.

Even at the time, this was an unfair characterization of Western bureaucracies. If bureaucrats really were out of control, public agencies would have been rife with corruption, but they were not in the 1970s, and they are not now. This is another fact that we should not take for granted. According to the anti-corruption group Transparency International, pervasive corruption is the reality in most countries. In those states, leaders struggle to deliver basic services, and citizens routinely pay bribes to get on with their daily lives. Such pervasive corruption has not been a problem in Western states for almost a century. Most people in the Western world go through their entire lives without paying a bribe to obtain a license or permit, or decent medical treatment, or a place for their child in school.

The decades following 1980 gave further reason for skepticism about the *Yes Minister* view of bureaucracy. These were hard years for public servants. Throughout the Western world, politicians experimented with a variety of techniques for tightening control over public agencies and increasing their efficiency. In many countries, senior public servants were required to compete against private sector executives for the right to hold top-level jobs. Job security for lower-level public servants was weakened as well. Public agencies were forced to hire contractors who employed cheaper, non-unionized workers. Entire sectors – schools, hospitals, prisons, airports, highways, bus and rail services, electrical and water utilities – were transferred to private operators. Those agencies that remained within government were publicly rated and ranked on their performance. Most Western countries adopted laws to break down secrecy in government offices.

There has been an active debate about how much money was saved, and how much the quality of service was improved, as a result of these reforms. The overall record is mixed: some reform experiments succeeded while others failed. But there can be no doubt about the overall effect of this broad reform movement. The comfortable bureaucratic world that was lampooned in *Yes Minister* had ceased to exist by the early 2000s. Austerity, competition and transparency were the new realities. The rate of growth in public sector employment in the advanced economies declined notably in the 1980s and turned negative in the 1990s. The global financial crisis gave further impetus to downsizing efforts in the governments of most advanced economies. In the United States, federal civilian employment in 2015 was essentially the same as in 1968, despite a 60 percent increase in population in that period. The impulses of the "budget-maximizing bureaucrat" had been contained quite effectively.

Conservatives in the 1970s were also skeptical about the capacity of democracies to avoid over-regulation and protectionism. These were two additional areas in which special interests appeared to have a lock on government policy. Well-organized industries, it was said, could "capture" regulatory agencies, and assure that regulatory powers were used to protect them from new competitors and technologies. Similarly, industry groups could preserve protective tariffs through lobbying and campaign contributions. It was hard to see how the power of special interests could be broken. In 1982, the economist Mancur Olson suggested that countries like the United Kingdom and the United States were condemned to suffer precisely because of their success in creating open and stable societies. This gave special interests the freedom and time to organize, which led inevitably to "institutional sclerosis" and economic stagnation.[8]

This dire prognosis was quickly disproved. By the end of the 1980s, experts were writing about a revolution in regulatory policy in the United States and Western Europe. Laws were overhauled to promote competition within key industries, even when established businesses protested intensely against the change. In Europe, regulatory functions were transferred to independent agencies that were structured much like central banks, so that they could make decisions without fear of meddling by politicians and special interests. Meanwhile, the project of trade liberalization intensified. The web of trade agreements that were negotiated after 1980 lowered tariffs and made it harder for politicians to raise them again. In effect, national leaders crafted another straitjacket that limited their capacity to appease domestic interests.

People who advance the overload thesis today suggest that the world has not changed much over the last forty years. Democracies, they say, still appear to suffer from some inherent flaw that drives them toward bloat and dysfunction. Politicians and voters, in this view, are incapable of doing much about this, since they are incapable of exercising self-control. As we can see, this view of the world is incorrect. The experience of the late 1960s and early 1970s did not reveal an *intrinsic* weakness in the democratic model. Conservatives of that era failed to recognize that Western governments are works in progress. They evolve in the light of experience. In the 1960s, the principle of self-rule was still a novelty in the West. The universal adult franchise was scarcely forty years old. Experts as well as ordinary people were confident about their capacity to take charge of the world around them:

after all, the allied powers had won a world war and revived their national economies. A certain degree of hubris and over-reach was perhaps inevitable.

The 1970s suggested the need for a course-correction. Conservatives were skeptical about the capacity of democratic systems to make such a correction. But time showed otherwise. Western states experimented with a raft of institutional reforms – independent central banks, fiscal rules, privatization of public services, weakening of union power, autonomous regulatory agencies, tougher free trade agreements – that addressed the "excess of democracy." Politicians and voters established constraints on their own authority, and changed the conventional wisdom about how a democratic state should be organized. Critics today argue that this course-correction has gone too far, and that some of the constraints imposed after the 1970s should now be loosened. That may well be the case. As we learned in the 1970s, there is no fixed formula for good governance. When circumstances change, so should institutions and laws.

6

Hard Choices Ahead

Government leaders craft strategies to pursue national objectives given the circumstances that confront them at a particular moment. Leaders want to believe that they have crafted an overall strategy that will work forever, a durable way of managing national problems. But leaders are always disappointed. Circumstances change and strategies have to be reconsidered and overhauled. This process of self-scrutiny and adaptation is unpleasant but unavoidable.

How will the circumstances confronting Western states change in coming decades, and how will governance strategies change as a consequence? We can only speculate. Here are four problems that seem likely to persist or intensify: terrorism, great power rivalries, economic inequality, and climate change. Each of these problems may confront leaders and citizens with a similar choice: between the construction of societies that are forward-looking and open, or defensive and closed. There are powerful pressures to follow the second route. A key challenge for leaders and citizens will be to resist those pressures and preserve the ideal of an open society.

The first of these problems, and perhaps the most tractable, is terrorism. Since the late 1990s, there has been a jump in the number of terrorist attacks in Western states by people who subscribe to a form of militant Islamic fundamentalism known as jihadism. The jihadi network is global: it includes well-organized groups based in fragile states as well as "lone wolves" living in immigrant enclaves in major cities of the West. The members of this network may differ on goals and tactics, but their motivations are broadly similar: anger over Western interference in Muslim countries; frustration over lack of opportunities for Muslim youth; and revulsion against the impiety and decadence of Western culture.

Jihadi terrorism has been portrayed as a "global epidemic" that is unprecedented and threatens the survival of Western states. This is not entirely correct. In fact, we are experiencing the third surge of terrorism since the late nineteenth century. Between the 1880s and early 1920s, Western countries struggled against an "international epidemic" of attacks by anarchist extremists. Anarchists killed the president of the United States and the president of France, and a half dozen other national leaders; they bombed theatres, parades, restaurants, and other civilian targets as well. There was a second "global epidemic" of terrorism in the 1970s, led by groups such as the Irish Republican Army, the Palestine Liberation Organization, the Japanese Red Army, Germany's Baader-Meinhof Group, Italy's Red Brigades, and the Weather Underground in the United States. These groups were connected in a loose international network that was supported by the Soviet Union and other Communist Bloc countries. They also killed civilians as well as politicians.

There are distinctive features to the current wave of jihadi terrorism. In particular, it plays on questions of faith and identity rather than class conflict or national self-determination. Otherwise, though, the challenge of containing terrorism is not new. Western societies are practiced in making the difficult choices between security and liberty that arise in the design of counterterrorism policies. Experience also shows that terrorism, when properly managed, is not an existential threat. No Western state faces political or social collapse because of terror attacks. Whether judged by the number of attacks or the number of deaths, the current wave of terrorism in North America and Western Europe is less severe than that of the 1970s.[1] Some experts observe that traffic accidents are a bigger threat to life in the West.[2]

This does not mean that the terrorist threat should be dismissed. Rather, the challenge is to craft a proportionate response. The purpose of terrorism, a Red Brigades leader wrote in 1968, is to goad the state into revealing its "reactionary essence."[3] Sometimes Western politicians take the bait. They elevate the terrorist threat into a "struggle to the death" over the survival of Western civilization.[4] Critics complain that the United States and some of its allies fell into this trap after the attacks of September 11, 2001. They began to construct "security states" that pursued extreme policies, including curtailment of civil liberties, pervasive surveillance, rigorous border controls, and a "global war" to eradicate the scourge of terrorism entirely. Such extreme measures, while viscerally satisfying, have limited effectiveness. Dogged police and intelligence work is a better long-term response.[5]

A second major problem that will preoccupy Western states in coming years is the revival of competition between great powers. In the 1990s, there were some experts who thought that the era of great power tensions was over. Europe was at peace, the Soviet Union had collapsed, and China was preoccupied with the internal problem of economic development. One writer famously celebrated "the end of history."[6] We know now that this was premature: we were only experiencing a brief lull in conflict between major states. Today, great power competition has revived.

Recently, the news has emphasized revived tensions between Russia and the United States. During the 1990s, Russian leaders were mainly concerned with re-establishing control within shrunken national borders. They could do little as the United States and its European allies wooed countries that had traditionally fallen within Russia's sphere of influence. Over the last fifteen years, however, Russian behavior has changed. An economic boom based on the export of fossil fuels has allowed Russia to rebuild its military, reassert control over neighboring territories, and claim a larger role in international affairs. Russian inter- ference in American and European elections is part of this project of reasserting global influence.

In the United States, Russia's resurgence has led to a revival of rhetoric from the early Cold

War. American conservatives decry Russia as the greatest threat facing American democracy, and call for a military build-up to contain Russian expansionism.[7] There are some signs of the resurgence of the "garrison mentality" that shaped American policy in the late 1940s and early 1950s. US policymakers worry about clandestine hacking of critical computer systems, just as they worried about infiltration of government agencies by "Red spies" sixty years ago.

In the long run, however, the revival of great power tensions is more likely to be tied to the rise of China. Russia's power hinges on the short-term profitability of energy exports. The Chinese economy is more robust, nearly ten times larger, and growing more rapidly. Chinese leaders have used their new wealth to finance a military build-up and recover the regional dominance that the country enjoyed centuries ago. China is determined to restore its standing in the world after decades of humiliation by other powers in the nineteenth and early twentieth centuries.

The political scientist Graham Allison points out that China's recent behavior is similar to that of the United States at the end of nineteenth century, as it emerged as the world's largest economy. Allison also worries about the potential for conflict between China and the United States. Throughout history, he says, the emergence of a new power has typically resulted in a violent clash with the established power. Today, China and the United States are said to be on a "collision course for war" unless leaders take "difficult and painful actions" to avoid it.[8] Indeed, some experts believe that the two countries are already locked in a "New Cold War." The United States began a "strategic pivot" of its military forces toward China a decade ago. US policymakers have also criticized China for targeting its institutions with cyber-attacks.[9]

A third problem confronting Western states is economic inequality. At first glance, this problem is also familiar. The low levels of inequality that were enjoyed in major Western countries in the three decades after World War II were a break from the historical pattern. Much of the rhetoric deployed in political fights today – about the rise of plutocracy and the "power of the one percent" – was introduced in the two decades preceding World War I, when inequality was even more severe than it is now.

Some experts believe the long-term prognosis for inequality in Western states is grim. The economist Branco Milanović has described a "perfect storm" of factors that could aggravate inequality in coming years.[10] These include the declining power of labor unions, the rising political influence of the rich, competition from low-wage workers abroad, the weakening of the social safety net, and the tendency of higher-income individuals to marry within their own income group.

The most important factor, however, is technological change. Advances in information and automation technologies are reducing the need for labor. Manufacturing and distribution is increasingly robotized, the internet has shuttered local stores and offices, and complex computer algorithms are replacing case management and judgment by professionals. We may be entering an era of jobless growth, in which the total value of production continues to expand, while the amount of work necessary to support production stagnates. In this world, a growing share of national income could be claimed by the owners of capital – that is, the people who finance the deployment of new technologies – while a smaller share is distributed broadly through salaries and wages.

There are several reasons to worry about rising inequality in income and wealth. One is a matter of justice: people ought to start their lives with roughly similar opportunities. There are also pragmatic considerations. Respect for government will decline if it seems to serve the rich alone. Peace and order could break down. The health of the economy will suffer if the mass of the population does not have enough income to purchase goods and services.

What can we do to reduce inequality, especially if it is driven by technological change? A conventional answer is to improve educational opportunities so that people can perform higher-skilled jobs. But that does not do much good when higher-skilled jobs are also threatened by computerization. Restoring the social safety net (healthcare, aid to the poor, pensions) helps on the edges, but does not get to the core of the problem, which is the diminishing supply of jobs. Many experts believe that a more effective response might be the introduction of a guaranteed minimum income (GMI): a regular payment from government financed by new taxes on wealth or a more progressive income tax.[11]

The GMI is not a new idea: President Richard Nixon proposed a form of it fifty years ago. But it is difficult to see how a GMI could be adopted anytime soon. It would require more taxing and spending, which would be at odds with the ethos of discipline and austerity that has prevailed for the last forty years. More profoundly, the GMI requires an adjustment of public attitudes about the meaning of labor. Western societies will not easily surrender the idea that people ought to work for their living.

Indeed, some people doubt that Western states will ever adopt policies as radical as a GMI. They suggest that countries will follow a darker path, which accepts growing inequality as an inescapable reality and attempts to contain the fallout. Milanović calls this "social separatism."[12] In this world, the economy would be oriented toward the production of goods and services favored by the rich, living in "fortress communities" protected by private guards. Public services – education, healthcare, parks, libraries, water and electricity – would be limited, and the political system would be twisted so that ordinary people could not demand more. Protest and disorder would be contained by tougher policing and expansion of the prison system.

The fourth problem that will confront Western states, and by far the most serious, is climate change. Evidence that the global climate is changing, and that this is caused in large part by human activity, is irrefutable. Since the dawn of the industrial revolution, people have burned ever-increasing amounts of fossil fuels – coal, oil, and gas – and released more carbon dioxide into the atmosphere. This build-up of carbon dioxide has impaired the release of heat from the planet into space, causing an increase in the temperature of the atmosphere. In 2014, an international panel estimated that the global mean temperature will increase by four degrees Celsius over pre-industrial levels by 2100 if current trends do not change.[13]

This much atmospheric warming will have catastrophic effects. Sea levels will rise, flooding coastal cities. Nations will be battered by extreme storms, droughts, and wildfires. Supplies of food and water will be jeopardized, possibly triggering wars over access to resources. In parts of the world where governments already struggle to maintain authority, social order might collapse entirely. The weakening of public institutions could lead to pandemics as well. Millions of people will migrate from devastated areas. The civil war in Syria and the outflow of refugees to Europe has been linked to drought caused by global warming. This could be an intimation of the dangers ahead.[14]

Solid evidence about climate change has been available for thirty years, but governments have dragged their feet in response. Leaders in democratic and non-democratic states worry that measures to curtail fuel consumption will dampen economic growth and weaken support for government. The leaders of established powers (such as the United States) are also reluctant to adopt growth-dampening policies if rivals (such as China) are not bound by similarly rigorous policies. But leaders of poorer countries say that rich countries ought to accept tougher restrictions, given that they have already benefited from decades of growth powered by fossil fuels. The international agreement on emissions control that was concluded in Paris in 2015 tried to manage these tensions. But according to many experts the commitments made in Paris were not big enough to ward off disaster. And even that agreement is jeopardized: in 2017, the administration of President Donald Trump announced that the United States would withdraw from the deal.

In some ways, the world has also suffered from bad luck. Expert opinion about climate change coalesced over a fifteen-year period, between the mid-1970s and the early 1990s. However, the world made other critical choices in that period. The advanced economies switched to a policy of limited government and economic liberalization, while China switched to a policy of rapid market-oriented growth. Governments became philosophically hostile to the kind of intensive regulation that is necessary to tackle climate change. And the vast global economy that emerged after the 1980s was "locked in" more tightly to fossil fuels. In China alone, the number of diesel- and gas-powered cars increased from two million in 1980 to 126 million in 2013.

Skeptics wonder whether governments will ever take the measures necessary to deal with climate change in a timely way. The more likely outcome, they suggest, is crisis government. After failing to take preventative measures, leaders will struggle with the effects of climate change. Power will be concentrated within the executive branch of government as leaders deal with one disaster after another. Police and military forces will be built up to maintain internal peace. Rich countries will tighten border controls in an attempt to block migration and the spread of disease. As international order breaks down, rich countries will engage more frequently in military action abroad to preserve access to oil and other resources.

Christian Parenti calls this a "politics of the armed lifeboat": a form of authoritarian government that deals with climate change by "arming, excluding, forgetting, repressing, policing, and killing."[15] There are others who believe that this dire outcome may arise even without taking climate change into account. James Kunstler has argued that the world may simply run out of oil and gas, triggering economic collapse and social chaos. At that moment, Kunstler suggests, central governments will pursue repressive and militaristic policies in a desperate attempt to maintain their authority.[16] The Australian scholars David Shearman and Joseph Smith suggest that the only way to avoid such catastrophes is by shifting immediately to some form of Platonic "rule by experts." Democracy, they say, has exhausted its usefulness. It will prove to be "but a moment in human history."[17]

We can see that these four problems – terrorism, great power conflict, inequality, and climate change – have a common feature. They seem to present people in Western countries with a similar choice. In every instance, we can imagine remedies that could preserve the essential features of an open society – such as tolerance, the free flow of people and ideas, respect for equal rights, and restraint in the use of governmental power. But we can also imagine responses that impinge radically on openness. These remedies emphasize the divide between people: between Christians and Muslims, between East and West, between rich and poor, and between citizens and aliens. Such remedies depend on the construction of walls between countries and within countries, on the concentration of executive power, and on police and soldiers to preserve order within borders.

Three considerations may push Western countries toward policies that undermine openness. The first is impatience. Policies that favor openness tend to require more time – to change beliefs, cultivate trust, and allow the impact of small adjustments in policy to accumulate. But voters sometimes demand immediate answers to major problems, and leaders sometimes indulge such demands. A second problem is delay in taking action. As time runs out, the problems become bigger and less tractable. Problem-solving gives way to crisis management.

A third consideration that militates against openness is simultaneity. All four of these problems will have to be dealt with at the same time. This raises the risk that they will all be dealt with in roughly similar ways. In any era, policymaking tends to be guided by a big idea or philosophy – what German philosophers have called the *zeitgeist*, or the spirit of the times. Over the last thirty years, for example, the big idea was economic liberalization and government retrenchment. The enthusiasm for "market solutions" permeated all aspects of governmental affairs – environmental protection, education, healthcare, and so on. We cannot be sure what the *zeitgeist* of the next thirty years will be. But it seems unlikely that we will end up addressing some problems by favoring openness and others by restricting openness. Overall, we are more likely to go one way or the other. If any one of these four problems tips into crisis, it might affect our attitude toward the other problems as well.

These four challenges are substantial. Even so, we should maintain some perspective. Preceding generations that lacked our advantages were compelled to overcome problems that seemed equally daunting at the time. The critical point is that we should resist the temptation to address these problems with quick but repressive governmental action. As a simple matter of justice in the treatment of people, this would be the wrong way to proceed. Hardline policies will corrode respect for government and weaken social stability in the long run. And as I shall argue in the final chapter, such policies also undermine the regenerative capacity of societies. By this, I mean the fundamental capacity of societies to reorganize themselves so that they can survive in a turbulent world.

7

Perestroika

In 1971, I was a young boy living in Pembroke, an old lumber town in the province of Ontario, Canada. My reading material included the 1953 edition of *Newnes' Pictorial Knowledge*, a British encyclopedia that had traveled to Canada with my parents in 1957. I had a subscription to *Soviet Life* magazine, which could be obtained for free from the embassy of the Soviet Union in Ottawa. Because I was a car enthusiast, I got myself on the mailing list of Rolls Royce, so the perquisites of capitalism were not forgotten entirely. And I had a paper route, delivering the Toronto *Globe and Mail* to neighbors every morning.

It was a difficult time in the West. The headlines in the *Globe and Mail* announced that the political and economic affairs of many countries were deeply troubled. In the autumn of 1970, the Canadian government briefly imposed a state of emergency in response to terrorist attacks. Shortly before that, soldiers had killed four students at an anti-war protest in Ohio. In August 1971, the US government abandoned the Bretton Woods currency system. *Newnes' Pictorial Knowledge* depicted Britain as a political and technological powerhouse, still basking in the afterglow of empire, but that seemed at odds with the realities of 1971. Rolls Royce went bankrupt that year.

By contrast, the Soviet Union was doing well, according to the glossy oversized pages of *Soviet Life*: there were bumper harvests, bustling factories, and great scientific advances. Soviet leaders gloated about their success in sidestepping the West's economic slump. Even in 1974, a very bad year for the global economy, Soviet national income was said to have grown by 4 percent, while in the West it stagnated.

A director of the Central Intelligence Agency in the 1970s later wrote: "I never heard a suggestion from the CIA, or the intelligence arms of the department of defense or state, that numerous Soviets recognized a growing, systemic economic problem."[1] A 1976 CIA analysis concluded that Soviet leaders faced no economic limits to a continued military build-up. The analysis noted the "unflagging persistence and patience" of Soviet leaders in "using the available means ... to strengthen themselves and weaken any prospective challengers."[2] The prevailing mood, one analyst recalled, was that "the Soviets were strong, and the United States was stuck in malaise."[3] If the Soviet Union had problems, it also had the capacity to address those problems creatively. It had "reformist potential."[4]

In fact, conditions in the Soviet Union were awful. When Mikhail Gorbachev became the country's leader in 1985, he said so. The path followed for seventy years was at a dead-end, Gorbachev declared: "new historical circumstances" required that the country "conduct matters in a new way ... in all spheres." This shift would require "an immense mobilization of creative forces."[5] Gorbachev called it *perestroika*, the Russian word for rebuilding or restructuring. At first, it seemed to go well. But Gorbachev lost control of events. Bureaucrats ignored instructions to change course. The Soviet grip on Poland and other neighboring states weakened. Territories within the Soviet Union pushed for autonomy. Gorbachev was almost toppled in a coup. Finally, in December 1991, the Soviet Union broke up, its powers scattered between Russia and fourteen other republics. The Soviet state was thrown on the ash heap of history. Russia still struggles to recover from this collapse.

Can Government Do Anything Right?

In a way, government is a sort of confidence trick. Confidence artists know two kinds of tricks: the "short con," a quick deception that yields a small reward, and the "long con," an elaborate ruse that involves many people and plays out over a long time.[6] Government is a long con. The aim is to persuade people that the state is durable and its authority is unassailable. ("Real power," Thomas Hobbes wrote in 1642, "accrues from a reputation for power."[7]) Maintaining peace and order must appear effortless. Power is cloaked in solemn rituals that are made to seem ancient. Public buildings are designed to convey solidity and permanence. If the confidence trick works, leaders benefit, because it discourages resistance to their authority. But the rest of us benefit too. If we do not believe that there is stability and predictability, we are reluctant to make plans and undertake new projects.

It is, though, still a confidence trick. Maintaining power is not effortless at all. Behind the scenes, leaders work furiously at operating the machinery of government in order to maintain the loyalty of citizens and the friendship of other states. During moments of stress, the curtain is drawn back and this activity is exposed, as it was in the Soviet Union between 1985 and 1991. These are moments of embarrassment for leaders. Maintaining power no longer looks effortless, and institutions and laws no longer seem immutable. Sometimes leaders lose control and the state collapses. This happens more often than we might recognize. Besides the Soviet Union, the ash heap of twentieth-century history contains dozens of other states as well.[8]

The job of holding a state together is especially difficult because the conditions of governance are constantly changing. Leaders craft a certain strategy for advancing the national interest, and develop a level of confidence about their mastery of the world around them. But then the world is unexpectedly altered. We have already noted some of the dimensions of changeability: demography, technology, patterns of commerce and finance, the structure of international politics, and climate. When conditions change, governance strategies have to be reconsidered, and laws and institutions amended.

In other words, all states must go through *perestroika*, although leaders may not explicitly acknowledge it. The Western democracies went through *perestroika* in the 1930s: we observed part of that process in Chapter 4. The method of governing Western states in 1948 was very different than it was in 1928. They went through *perestroika* again in the 1970s, as we noted in Chapter 5. The method of governing in 1995 was very different than in 1975. And we are going through *perestroika* today: the method of governing in 2027 will be very different than in 2007. One of the unappreciated virtues of Western states is their ability to undertake *perestroika* and survive.

We can make some general observations about the way *perestroika* works in Western democracies. There is a pattern. Before the process begins, there is a generally accepted view about the role of government in everyday life. In the last chapter, I called this the *zeitgeist* or the spirit of the times. Others have called it the public philosophy, or the policy paradigm, or the conventional wisdom. An imperfect label for the public philosophy in 1928 is laissez-fairism; in 1975, welfare-state Keynesianism; in 2007, disciplined-state globalism. However, there is inevitably a point at which confidence in the conventional wisdom starts to break down. The usual policies no longer produce the expected results. A great shock or failure – the crash of 1929, Britain's IMF crisis of 1976, the financial crisis of 2007–8 – may accelerate the collapse in confidence.

At this point, democracies slide into a funk. There is a general feeling that governments and societies have lost their way. People look enviously at non-democratic regimes that appear to perform better. In the doldrums that preceded World War I,

Woodrow Wilson admired the efficiency of Imperial Germany. In 1933, many people lauded Benito Mussolini, the Fascist dictator of Italy. (President Franklin Roosevelt said he was "deeply impressed" by Mussolini's accomplishments.) In the 1970s, some envied Russia, and others Japan, where democracy was kept on a tighter leash. Today, we look at China. But there are two difficulties with such comparisons. The first is that we are easily misled when we look at authoritarian systems, because it is difficult to see what is going on inside them. This is what happened with regard to the Soviet Union in the 1970s. The second is that we look only at short-term performance. The strategies pursued by authoritarian leaders might be effective in addressing the challenges immediately before them, but the critical question is whether they can alter those strategies when they no longer work. In other words, can their regimes launch *perestroika* and survive?

When confidence in the conventional wisdom collapses in Western democracies, a feeling of drift takes hold. There is a sense that nothing is being done to regain control of events. This is a misperception. Throughout society, the search begins for new ideas. Intellectuals, interest groups, and aspiring politicians formulate and test new platforms and slogans. National and sub-national governments experiment with new policies. Many of these innovations fail, but a few new ideas take hold. A coherent alternative program takes shape. It begins as a fringe movement but eventually reaches the mainstream. Over several elections, a new cadre of leaders, supporters of the emerging paradigm, displaces the old cadre. At the end, institutions and laws are amended, and a new conventional wisdom about the role of government is established.

This is how *perestroika* works in democracies. It is not formally announced or centrally planned. It is a societal project, the spontaneous and collective effort of people inside and outside government. It also takes time. Two decades passed between the crash of 1929 and the general acceptance by conservative opposition parties of the new approach, eventually known as welfare-state Keynesianism. Similarly, the shift toward disciplined-state globalism begun by Ronald Reagan and Margaret Thatcher at the end of the 1970s was not really completed until 1996. In that year, Democratic President Bill Clinton publicly declared an end to the "era of big government," while the Labour Party led by Tony Blair published a manifesto praising free markets and globalization.

If history is a guide, the United States and the United Kingdom are only halfway through the current round of *perestroika*, which probably began after the global financial crisis of 2007–8. The pre-crisis paradigm has been widely discredited. A new paradigm has not yet emerged, although there are hints about the themes it might emphasize. In the meantime, politics is fraught with false starts and U-turns. There are no stable governing coalitions. Short-lived minority governments are more common. Politics will probably be like this for several more years, until the ship of state reaches calmer water. This phase will be unpleasant, but the larger point should not be forgotten. At the end, Western states will have undergone *perestroika* and survived. Many states cannot do this. They lack the adaptive capacity that is essential to long-run survival.

A particular set of institutional and cultural arrangements are essential to adaptive capacity in Western democracies. The institutional features include freedom of speech, a healthy community of independent media and interest groups, easy access to information held by government agencies, a significant degree of political decentralization, and open competition for leadership positions. The cultural features include pragmatism, empiricism, and open-mindedness. These are the qualities of an open society. When they are combined, they turn whole societies into powerful engines for inventing and testing new ideas about government. Under such conditions, *perestroika* is a problem for everyone, not simply statesmen and bureaucrats. Non-democratic regimes like China toy with some of these arrangements but do not commit to all of them. This allows for short-term stability and efficiency but undermines long-term adaptability.

Hence another reason for being careful about our responses to the four problems outlined in the preceding chapter. We can imagine how governments could respond to each of those problems – or the combination of all four – by retreating from the commitment to an open society. The immediate emphasis would be on security and crisis management; this would be done by concentrating executive power, limiting protest and dissent, and building walls to staunch the flow of people and ideas. Our societies might feeler safer for the moment, but they would also be more brittle. They would be less adroit at restructuring when history brings us to the next turn in the road.

There is, perhaps, one change in attitude that can help us work through the current malaise and prepare for the road ahead. This relates to our understanding about human progress. The expectation that there will be constant progress is peculiar to the modern age. Machiavelli, for example, thought that history worked in cycles: that democracies were inevitably transformed into dictatorships, then to oligarchies, then to democracies again, in perpetuity.[9] In the last few centuries, we have operated on the principle that life should generally get better over time. And in the decades after World War II – years of unusual peace, prosperity, and innovation – perhaps we acquired the more extreme idea that progress should be relentless, that every step in the journey should be forward.

This is an unreasonable conception of how the world ought to work. It makes politics more difficult, because every setback is construed as a catastrophe, as a sign that the great project of self-government has failed. There are people who talk like this today. It would be healthier and more realistic to acknowledge that there will be setbacks. There will always be events that require us to regain our footing. Having said this, we should take the long view and acknowledge how far we have come. Two hundred years ago, it was difficult to envisage states composed of tens of millions of people (and in a few cases, hundreds of millions) that are stable, peaceful, prosperous, democratic, respectful of the rule of law, and attentive to human rights. Government has done that right, and it is no small thing.

Further Reading

A good review of the current state of politics is provided by: John B. Judis, *The Populist Explosion: How the Great Recession Transformed American and European Politics* (New York: Columbia Global Reports, 2016). For an introduction to the state system, see: John L. Campbell and John A. Hall, *The World of States* (London: Bloomsbury, 2015). This book adapts the concept of grand strategy, used in the field of International Relations. For an overview of that concept, see Hal Brands, *What Good is Grand Strategy? Power and Purpose in American Statecraft* (Ithaca, NY: Cornell University Press, 2014). A classical statement of the challenges of statecraft is provided by Niccolò Machiavelli, *The Prince* (Chicago: University of Chicago Press, 1985).

For a thorough discussion of the long-term decline of violence in Western societies, see Steven

Further Reading

Pinker, *The Better Angels of Our Nature: Why Violence Has Declined* (New York: Viking, 2011). The evolution of European states is described by Charles Tilly, *Coercion, Capital, and European States, AD 990–1992* (Oxford: Blackwell, 1992). The emergence of modern-day "civilian states" in Europe is described by James J. Sheehan, *The Monopoly of Violence: Why Europeans Hate Going to War* (London: Faber and Faber, 2008). On recent developments in the European Union, see George Friedman, *Flashpoints: The Emerging Crisis in Europe* (London: Scribe, 2015). For a quick introduction to the challenges of sectionalist politics, read John F. Kennedy, *Profiles in Courage* (New York: Harper, 1956). A good overview of the evolution of US foreign policy is provided in David Milne, *Worldmaking: The Art and Science of American Diplomacy* (New York: Farrar, Straus and Giroux, 2015). On the changes in US domestic and foreign security policy after the 9/11 attacks, see my book *The Collapse of Fortress Bush: The Crisis of Authority in American Government* (New York: New York University Press, 2008).

The following books are all helpful in understanding why legitimacy matters, and how it is established in Western states: Robert Jackson,

Sovereignty: The Evolution of an Idea (Cambridge: Polity, 2013); M. J. C. Vile, *Constitutionalism and the Separation of Powers*, 2nd edn (Indianapolis: Liberty Fund, 1998); Tom Bingham, *The Rule of Law* (London: Allen Lane, 2010); Jack Donnelly, *Universal Human Rights in Theory and Practice*, 3rd edn (Ithaca, NY: Cornell University Press, 2013).

An excellent overview of the long-term development of the global economy is provided by Robert Marks, *The Origins of the Modern World: A Global and Environmental Narrative from the Fifteenth to the Twenty-First Century*, 3rd edn (Lanham, MD: Rowman & Littlefield, 2015). For a detailed discussion of economic developments in the last century, see Jeffrey A. Frieden, *Global Capitalism: Its Fall and Rise in the Twentieth Century* (New York: Norton, 2006), and also Robert Gilpin, *Global Political Economy: Understanding the International Economic Order* (Princeton, NJ: Princeton University Press, 2001). An interesting discussion of recent concerns about the threats to sovereignty and security that may be posed by economic integration is provided in: Joshua Kurlantzick, *State Capitalism: How the Return of Statism is Transforming the World* (New York: Oxford University Press, 2016).

Further Reading

For a survey of the economic and social turmoil of the 1970s, see Thomas Borstelmann, *The 1970s: A New Global History* (Princeton, NJ: Princeton University Press, 2012). Chapter 5 also draws on my book *The Logic of Discipline: Global Capitalism and the New Architecture of Government* (New York: Oxford University Press, 2010). For a thorough review of public management reforms in the United Kingdom after 1980, see Christopher Hood and Ruth Dixon, *A Government That Worked Better and Cost Less?* (New York: Oxford University Press, 2015). The UK was often regarded as a leader in public sector restructuring.

Chapter 6 addresses the challenges of great power rivalry, terrorism, inequality, and carbon shock. For good introductions to these topics, see: Graham T. Allison, *Destined for War: Can America and China Escape Thucydides's Trap?* (Boston, MA: Houghton Mifflin Harcourt, 2017); Petter Nesser, *Islamist Terrorism in Europe: A History* (New York: Oxford University Press, 2015); Branko Milanović, *Global Inequality: A New Approach for the Age of Globalization* (Cambridge, MA: The Belknap Press, 2016); Martin Ford, *Rise of the Robots: Technology and the Threat of a Jobless Future* (New York: Basic Books, 2015); Nigel M. de S. Cameron, *Will Robots Take Your Job?* (Cambridge:

Polity, 2017); and Andrew T. Guzman, *Overheated: The Human Cost of Climate Change* (New York: Oxford University Press, 2013).

Chapter 7 summarizes an argument about the adaptability of democratic systems that I make in *Four Crises of American Democracy* (New York: Oxford University Press, 2017).

Notes

Chapter 1 Why is Everyone so Angry?

1 Paul Krugman, "Our Unknown Country," *New York Times*, November 8, 2016. Francis Fukuyama, "America: The Failed State," *Prospect*, December 13, 2017.
2 Gideon Rachman, "The Crisis in Anglo-American Democracy," *Financial Times*, August 22, 2016.
3 Roberto Stefan Foa and Yascha Mounk, "The Democratic Disconnect," *Journal of Democracy* 27, no. 3 (2016): 5–17.
4 Munich Security Conference, *Munich Security Report 2017: Post-Truth, Post-West, Post-Order?* (Munich: Munich Security Conference, 2017), 5.
5 Executive Office of the President, *National Security Strategy of the United States* (Washington, DC: Executive Office of the President, September 17, 2002), iv.
6 John Dewey, *The Public and Its Problems* (New York: H. Holt and Company, 1927), Chapter 1.

Notes

Chapter 2 The Long Peace

1 Jason K. Stearns, *Dancing in the Glory of Monsters: The Collapse of the Congo and the Great War of Africa* (New York: PublicAffairs, 2011), 4–5.

2 John Lewis Gaddis, *The Long Peace: Inquiries into the History of the Cold War* (New York: Oxford University Press, 1987). In 2016, the Danish writer Janne Teller published a short book that invited readers to imagine what it would be like to live through a European war: Janne Teller, *War: What If It Were Here?* (London: Simon & Schuster UK Ltd., 2016). Fifty years ago, such a book would have been unnecessary.

3 Caelainn Barr, "Figures Put Europe's Summer of Violence in Context," *Guardian*, July 28, 2016.

4 Steven Pinker, *The Better Angels of Our Nature: Why Violence Has Declined* (New York: Viking, 2011), xii.

5 Charles Tilly, *Coercion, Capital, and European States, AD 990–1992* (Oxford: Blackwell, 1992), Table 3.1.

6 Solemn Declaration on European Union, June 19, 1983.

7 Frederick Jackson Turner, "The Significance of the Section in American History," *Wisconsin Magazine of History* 8, no. 3 (1925): 255–80, 271, 279; Frederick Jackson Turner, Max Farrand, and Avery Craven, *The Significance of Sections in American History* (New York: H. Holt and Company, 1932), 9, 14.

116

8 Commencement Address at Yale University, June 11, 1962, http://www.presidency.ucsb.edu/ws/?pid=29661.

9 Telegram from President Dwight D. Eisenhower to Senator Richard B. Russell, September 27, 1957, http://www.presidency.ucsb.edu/ws/?pid=10913.

10 Jari Eloranta, "From the Great Illusion to the Great War: Military Spending Behaviour of the Great Powers, 1870–1913," *European Review of Economic History* 11, no. 2 (2007): 255–83, Table 1.

11 John F. Kennedy, Inaugural Address, January 20, 1961, http://www.presidency.ucsb.edu/ws/index.php?pid=8032&.

12 William C. Martel, *Grand Strategy in Theory and Practice: The Need for an Effective American Foreign Policy* (New York: Cambridge University Press, 2015), 351.

Chapter 3 The Right to Rule

1 United Nations Resolutions 1378 (November 14, 2001) and 1973 (March 17, 2011).

2 Quoted in Quentin Skinner, *The Foundations of Modern Political Thought*, 2 vols (Cambridge: Cambridge University Press, 1978), I.285.

3 Thomas Hobbes, *On the Citizen* (Cambridge: Cambridge University Press, 1998), Chapter 15.

4 Albert V. Dicey, *Introduction to the Study of the Law of the Constitution*, 3rd edn (London: Macmillan, 1889), 151, 167.

5 Khalilah Brown-Dean et al., *Fifty Years of the Voting*

Rights Act: The State of Race in Politics (Washington, DC: Joint Center for Political and Economic Studies, 2015), 8–11.

6 Francis Fukuyama, "America in Decay," *Foreign Affairs* 93, no. 5 (2014): 3–26.

7 Mark Blumenthal, "The Underpinnings of Trump's Approval Ratings," *SurveyMonkey Election Tracking Blog* (2017).

8 Pew Global Indicators Database, "How satisfied are you with the country's direction?," http://www. pewglobal.org/database/indicator/3/survey/all.

9 Howard W. French, *Everything Under the Heavens: How the Past Helps Shape China's Push for Global Power* (New York: Alfred A. Knopf, 2017), Chapter 1.

Chapter 4 Taming the Economy

1 Timothy Mitchell, *Carbon Democracy* (New York: Verso, 2011), 124; Alasdair Roberts, *Four Crises of American Democracy: Representation, Mastery, Discipline, Anticipation* (New York: Oxford University Press, 2017), 86–7.

2 John F. Kennedy, Commencement Address at Yale University, June 11, 1962, http://www.presidency. ucsb.edu/ws/?pid=29661.

3 Walter W. Heller, *New Dimensions of Political Economy* (Cambridge, MA: Harvard University Press, 1966).

4 Kenichi Ohmae, *The End of the Nation State: The Rise of Regional Economies* (New York: Free Press, 1995), 11.

Notes

5 Susan Strange, *The Retreat of the State: The Diffusion of Power in the World Economy* (New York: Cambridge University Press, 1996), 3.

6 I discuss this in more detail in Alasdair Roberts, *The End of Protest: How Free-Market Capitalism Learned to Control Dissent* (Ithaca, NY: Cornell University Press, 2013), Chapter 3.

7 Daniel W. Drezner, *The System Worked: How the World Stopped Another Great Depression* (New York: Oxford University Press, 2014).

8 Francis Fukuyama, "The End of History?," *National Interest* 16, no. 3 (1989): 3–16.

9 Andrea Willige, "The World's Top Economy: The US vs China in Five Charts," Geneva: World Economic Forum, December 5, 2016, https://www.weforum.org/agenda/2016/12/the-world-s-top-economy-the-us-vs-china-in-five-charts.

10 Adam Watson, *The Evolution of International Society: A Comparative Historical Analysis* (London: Routledge, 2009), 232.

Chapter 5 The Battle of the Bulge

1 John Micklethwait and Adrian Wooldridge, *The Fourth Revolution: The Global Race to Reinvent the State* (New York: Penguin Press, 2014), 21, 87, 222, 251.

2 James Reston, "The Crisis of Democracy," *New York Times*, June 29, 1975.

3 Michel Crozier, Samuel P. Huntington, and Joji Watanuki, *The Crisis of Democracy* (New York: New York University Press, 1975), 2.

4 Roberts, *Four Crises of American Democracy*, 98.
5 Micklethwait and Wooldridge, *The Fourth Revolution*, 177.
6 Paul Bowles and Gordon White, "Central Bank Independence," *Journal of Development Studies* 31, no. 2 (1994): 235–64, 243.
7 James Saturno and Megan Lynch, *A Balanced Budget Constitutional Amendment: Background and Congressional Options* (Washington, DC: Congressional Research Service, December 20, 2011), 11, 26.
8 Mancur Olson, *The Rise and Decline of Nations* (New Haven: Yale University Press, 1982), 77, 87.

Chapter 6 Hard Choices Ahead

1 Comparing the annual average number of attacks and fatalities in 1996–2015 to the average in the 1970s. Data is collected within the Global Terrorism Database, https://www.start.umd.edu/gtd.
2 Christopher Michaelsen, "The Triviality of Terrorism," *Australian Journal of International Affairs* 66, no. 4 (2012): 431–49, 437; Jessica Wolfendale, "The Narrative of Terrorism as an Existential Threat," in *Routledge Handbook of Critical Terrorism Studies*, ed. Richard Jackson, (New York: Routledge, 2016), 114–23, 116.
3 Milton Meltzer, *The Terrorists* (New York: Harper & Row, 1983), 144, 166.
4 Michaelsen, "The Triviality of Terrorism," 431.
5 Seth G. Jones and Martin C. Libicki, *How Terrorist*

Groups End (Santa Monica, CA: RAND Corporation, 2008), 121–39.

6 Francis Fukuyama, *The End of History and the Last Man* (New York: Free Press, 2006).

7 In May 2017, Senator John McCain said that Russia was "the far greatest challenge that we have," http://fortune.com/2017/05/29/john-mccain-isis-vladimir-putin.

8 Graham T. Allison, *Destined for War: Can America and China Escape Thucydides's Trap?* (Boston, MA: Houghton Mifflin Harcourt, 2017), vii.

9 Director of National Intelligence, Statement on the Worldwide Threat Assessment of the US Intelligence Community, May 11, 2017.

10 Branko Milanović, *Global Inequality: A New Approach for the Age of Globalization* (Cambridge, MA: The Belknap Press, 2016), 181.

11 A summary of policy options is provided by Martin Ford, *Rise of the Robots: Technology and the Threat of a Jobless Future* (New York: Basic Books, 2015), Chapter 10. The case for a wealth tax is presented by Thomas Piketty, *Capital in the Twenty-First Century* (Cambridge, MA: The Belknap Press, 2014), Chapter 15.

12 Milanović, *Global Inequality*, 198. See also Peter Frase, *Four Futures: Life after Capitalism* (London: Verso, 2016), Chapter 4.

13 Intergovernmental Panel on Climate Change, *Climate Change 2014: Synthesis Report* (Geneva: Intergovernmental Panel of Climate Change, 2014), 9. Other gases also contribute to global warming,

but for simplicity I focus on the main culprit, carbon dioxide.

14 Colin P. Kelley et al., "Climate Change in the Fertile Crescent and Implications of the Recent Syrian Drought," *Proceedings of the National Academy of Sciences* 112, no. 11 (2015): 3241–6.

15 Christian Parenti, *Tropic of Chaos: Climate Change and the New Geography of Violence* (New York: Nation Books, 2011), 11.

16 James Kunstler, *The Long Emergency: Surviving the Converging Catastrophes of the Twenty-First Century* (London: Atlantic, 2005), Chapter 7. Other experts say that Kunstler exaggerates the risk of exhausting fossil fuel supplies.

17 David J.C. Shearman and Joseph Wayne Smith, *The Climate Change Challenge and the Failure of Democracy* (Westport, CT: Praeger, 2007), 15.

Chapter 7 Perestroika

1 Stansfield Turner, "Intelligence for a New World Order," *Foreign Affairs* 70, no. 4 (1991): 150–66.

2 Central Intelligence Agency, *Intelligence Community Experiment in Competitive Analysis: Soviet Strategic Objectives* (Washington, DC: Central Intelligence Agency, 1976), 3 and 23.

3 Bruce D. Berkowitz, "U.S. Intelligence Estimates of the Soviet Collapse: Reality and Perception," *International Journal of Intelligence and CounterIntelligence* 21, no. 2 (2008): 237–50, 241.

4 Stephen F. Cohen, *Sovieticus: American Perceptions*

Notes

and Soviet Realities (New York: Norton, 1986), 25, 83.

5 Speeches at the Commemoration of the Great Patriotic War, May 8, 1985, and to the Leningrad Party Organization, May 17, 1985.

6 "How 'Con Men' Operate," *Kansas City Star*, April 4, 1921, 6.

7 Hobbes, *On the Citizen*, Chapter 15.

8 A list of former states is provided on Wikipedia, https://en.wikipedia.org/wiki/List_of_former_ sovereign_states.

9 Niccolò Machiavelli, *The Essential Writings of Machiavelli* (New York: Modern Library, 2007), 116.